Nick Vandome

Alexa
for Seniors

In easy steps is an imprint of In Easy Steps Limited
16 Hamilton Terrace · Holly Walk · Leamington Spa
Warwickshire · United Kingdom · CV32 4LY
www.ineasysteps.com

Notice of Liability
Every effort has been made to ensure that this book contains accurate
and current information. However, In Easy Steps Limited and the
author shall not be liable for any loss or damage suffered by readers
as a result of any information contained herein.

Trademarks
All trademarks are acknowledged as belonging to their respective
companies.

In Easy Steps Limited supports The Forest Stewardship Council (FSC),
the leading international forest certification organization. All our titles
that are printed on Greenpeace approved FSC certified paper carry the
FSC logo.

MIX
Paper from
responsible sources
FSC® C020837

Printed and bound in the United Kingdom

ISBN 978-1-84078-907-2

Contents

8 Communicating 135

9 Online Shopping 147

10 Alexa and the Smart Home 153

1 Introducing Alexa

The digital voice assistant, Alexa, is fast becoming a fixture in many households. This chapter looks at getting started with Alexa.

About Alexa and the Echo

Alexa has become synonymous with smart speakers in the home. These are devices that react to voice commands and can perform a variety of useful tasks: from playing music, to setting reminders, to providing weather reports.

Alexa and its smart speaker are both Amazon products, and the first thing to remember about Alexa and the smart speaker is that they are two different entities:

- **Alexa** is the digital voice assistant that provides the information through the smart speaker.

- The smart speaker itself is known as the **Echo**, and this is the physical device that provides a home for Alexa. There are several different models of Echo, and they all operate with Alexa.

Don't forget

Echo devices can be bought from the Amazon website.

The services and information delivered through the Amazon Echo by Alexa are cloud-based, which means that all of the data is stored in an Amazon computer (server) and then delivered through the Amazon Echo when it is requested. Nothing is physically stored on the Echo – it is merely a delivery system. The Echo works through connecting to your home Wi-Fi network: without Wi-Fi it will not function properly.

Alexa can react to different people's voices, and some of the uses for the Echo and Alexa include:

- Setting reminders for important tasks such as taking regular medication, paying bills, and birthdays of family and friends. This can be done by creating daily or weekly reminders using Alexa or the Alexa app.

- Performing a range of organizational tasks, such as creating appointments and making lists. Appointments will be announced by Alexa at the relevant time.

- Playing music from a range of sources: from the radio to Amazon's own music library.

- Getting the latest news, weather, sport, and much more in a daily briefing. This can be activated with a single command once it has been set up.

- Calling or messaging family and friends on their smartphones, or anyone who also has an Echo device or the Alexa app.

- Sending announcements to Alexa on an Echo device, which will be spoken from the device. It is also possible to communicate between multiple Echo devices within the same home.

- Playing games and finding entertainment options such as the latest movie listings.

- Making online purchases on Amazon.

- Controlling smart home devices such as smart lights and smart heating. This can involving turning items on and off and also setting customized routines to control smart home devices when you are away from home.

- Creating customized routines whereby a range of different tasks can be performed using a single voice command.

For more information about obtaining the Alexa app and using it to set up an Echo device, see pages 14-19.

For more details about online shopping using voice commands, see Chapter 9.

Models of Echo

There are several different models of Echo, which provide different functionality. This gives you the flexibility of putting different Echo models in different rooms of your home, to create the ultimate Echo experience. The models of the Echo include:

- **Echo**. Now in its third generation, this is the original version of the device and can be considered as the "standard" Echo. It is a high-quality speaker that provides excellent sound for music, in addition to the full range of services from Alexa. It comes in a range of colors, and fabric covers can also be placed over the device so that it can blend in to any room in your home. The cover style can be selected when you buy the Echo from Amazon.

The top ring on the Echo glows blue when Alexa is dealing with a voice command. The controls at the top of the Echo are volume up and down (top and bottom buttons), mute the microphone (left-hand button), and the action button (right-hand button) that can be used to set up Wi-Fi.

Don't forget

The volume on the Echo can also be changed with a voice command, such as: "Alexa, volume up 1".

Beware

If the top ring is red, this means that the microphone has been turned off and Alexa is not actively listening for commands.

- **Echo Dot**. This is a smaller version of the standard Echo device, and is a good option if you want to expand your Echo system so that you have several devices in different rooms. If you choose to do this, each Echo can be used independently – e.g. you can play different music in the family room and a bedroom, using a family plan from a compatible service such as Amazon Music.

Two Echo Dots can be paired together to create stereo sound when playing music.

There are different versions of the Dot, including one that displays a clock on its side:

...cont'd

Hot tip

If you have the Amazon Prime service, this will enable you to watch Prime Video movies and TV shows on the Echo Show. Other benefits of Amazon Prime are one-day delivery on qualifying Amazon products, free downloads on selected books, and reduced prices on video rentals (although there is also a large range of free video items).

- **Echo Show**. This is a model of the Echo that comes with a display screen of either 5.5 inches or 8 inches (measured diagonally). It can be used for all of the same functions as the standard Echo, plus it can be used to stream movies and TV shows, and make video calls.

- **Echo Studio**. This is a version of the Echo that is designed with music lovers in mind. It is a high-fidelity speaker that includes five individual speakers for an immersive sound experience. It also manages to include all of the standard Alexa functions.

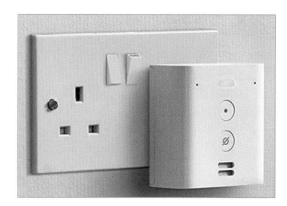

- **Echo Plus**. This is the largest Echo model and contains a built-in smart home hub, so it is an excellent option if you want to use it to control other Echo devices and also smart devices in the home (although much of this can also be done with the standard Echo).

- **Echo Flex**. This is the most mobile of the Echo devices as it can be easily plugged into any power socket. It is ideal for accessing information from Alexa such as weather forecasts or traffic reports, and also controlling smart home devices such as lighting or heating.

Hot tip

The Echo Flex cannot be used to play music, but it can be connected to an external speaker for playing music, using a cable or Bluetooth.

- **Echo Wall Clock**. This has to be used with another Echo device, and can display a number of timers as well as the time.

Hot tip

The Echo Wall Clock is a good option to use in the kitchen: timers can be set on the main Echo device and viewed on the Wall Clock if you need a timer while cooking.

Giving Alexa a Voice

The Echo smart speaker, and other compatible Amazon devices such as the Amazon Fire TV stick, is where Alexa receives voice commands and issues replies. On its own the Echo is virtually useless: it needs the Alexa app to set it up so that it can function. The Alexa app performs a number of tasks in relation to the Echo but the first one is to set it up, ready for use. This involves downloading the Alexa app and setting it up too. To do this:

For more information about using the Alexa app, see Chapter 3.

The Alexa app can be used on Apple devices – e.g. the iPhone and the iPad – and also Android smartphones and tablets. Download the Alexa app from the Apple App Store for Apple devices, or from the Google Play Store for Android devices.

An Amazon account can also be set up on the Amazon website.

1 Open the relevant app store and enter **alexa app** into the Search box. Tap on the **Get** button (Apple) or the **Install** button (Google) to download the app

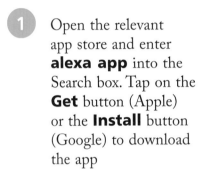
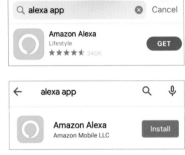

2 Tap on the app to open it and sign in to the app

3 An Amazon account is required to use the Alexa app. If you already have one, enter your sign-in details and tap on the **Sign-In** button. If you do not have an account, tap on the **Create a New Amazon Account** button to create one

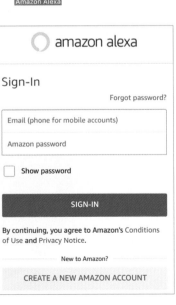

4 Tap on your own name or, if it is for another user, tap on the **I'm someone else** button

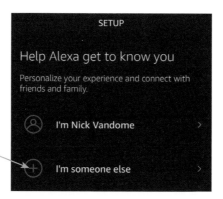

5 The name used by the Alexa app is displayed. Change this, if required, and tap on the **Continue** button

6 To enable the Alexa app on a smartphone to send and receive calls and messages with an Echo device, enter the smartphone's number and tap on the **Continue** button to complete the Alexa app setup

The name displayed in Step 4 is taken from your Amazon account details.

Items such as the display name and the smartphone number can be edited or added after the setup process has been completed. This is done within the Alexa app settings. See pages 42-47 for details.

15

Setting Up an Echo Device

Once the Alexa app has been downloaded and set up, it can be used for setting up an Echo device. To do this:

Don't forget

The Alexa app can be used to communicate with a range of different devices, not just the Echo. For instance, if you have smart lighting installed in your home, the Alexa app can be connected to this too. If this is the case, there will be an option to select the smart lighting system in Step 4. See Chapter 10 for more details about using smart home devices.

1. Open the Amazon Alexa app on a smartphone or tablet

2. Plug in the Amazon Echo. Alexa will tell you when it is ready to be set up. Tap on this button to access the **Menu** options

3. Tap on the **Add Device** button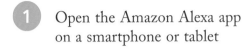

4. Tap on the **Amazon Echo** icon to add an Echo device. (Other types of devices can also be added here – see tip)

5. Tap on the type of Echo device to be added

6 Ensure that the Echo is plugged in and tap on the **Yes** button if the Echo is displaying an orange light around the perimeter at the top of the device

Is your Echo plugged in and displaying an orange light?

Once your Echo is plugged in, the light will turn orange after about a minute.

YES

NO

7 The Bluetooth option on the smartphone or tablet on which the Alexa app is being used has to be turned **On** so that it can communicate with the Echo device. Tap on the **Settings** button to go to the relevant settings within your smartphone or tablet

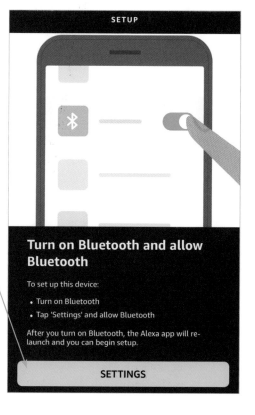

SETUP

Turn on Bluetooth and allow Bluetooth

To set up this device:

• Turn on Bluetooth
• Tap 'Settings' and allow Bluetooth

After you turn on Bluetooth, the Alexa app will re-launch and you can begin setup.

SETTINGS

Don't forget

Bluetooth has to be turned **On** for the smartphone or tablet that is using the Alexa app, before it can link to the Echo.

...cont'd

8 The settings should open at the Amazon Alexa section. Drag the **Bluetooth** button to **On**

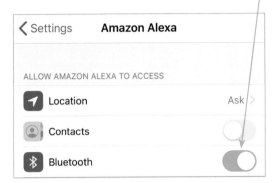

Without Wi-Fi the Echo will not be able to function.

9 Return to the Alexa app, which should be ready to continue the setup process. Tap on the **Continue** button

An Echo can be set up.

By tapping "Continue", you agree to Amazon's Conditions of Use and Terms.

LATER   CONTINUE

10 Since Alexa is a cloud-based service, it needs access to the internet via your home Wi-Fi network. Tap on the required network

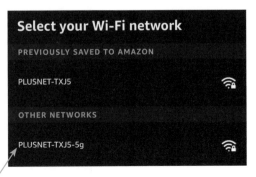

Select your Wi-Fi network

PREVIOUSLY SAVED TO AMAZON

PLUSNET-TXJ5

OTHER NETWORKS

PLUSNET-TXJ5-5g

11 Enter the password for your Wi-Fi router, and tap on the **Connect** button to enable the Echo to join the Wi-Fi network

The password for the Wi-Fi router should be located on the router itself (usually on the back or the bottom), or on a card that comes with the router.

12 A confirmation message is displayed when the Echo has connected to the Wi-Fi network. Tap on the **Continue** button

19

13 Once the Echo has been connected to the Wi-Fi network, it will be able to communicate with the

It is optional to assign a room to the Echo, but it can be useful if you have more than one Echo device in your home, so that you can easily identify each one.

Alexa app. It is also possible to assign a specific room for the Echo. Tap on a room and tap on the **Continue** button to complete the setup process

Echo Lights

The standard Echo and the Echo Dot have a ring around the top of the device. This is used to display colors to indicate various states of the device – e.g. listening to a command or being ready for Wi-Fi to be set up. The colored light rings on the standard Echo and Echo Dot include:

When Alexa is processing a command, the light ring is blue with cyan spinning around it. If the light ring alternates between blue and cyan, this means that Alexa is responding to a command.

- **Orange light**. This is the state of the light ring during the initial setup process, when Alexa is ready to be connected to a Wi-Fi network. It is also the color of the ring if you change the Wi-Fi network, or there are network problems.

- **Blue light**. This is the state of the light ring when Alexa is listening to a command after the wake word has been spoken. The small section of cyan light indicates the direction from where the command has come.

For details about changing the wake word for Alexa, see page 49.

- **Red light**. This is the state of the light ring when the microphone has been turned off and Alexa is not in listening mode – i.e. voice commands cannot be actioned.

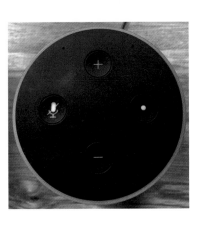

- **Green pulsing light**. This is the state of the light ring when there is an incoming call to the Echo.

- **Yellow pulsing light**. This is the state of the light ring when a message has been sent to the Echo and it is ready to play.

For more information about using Alexa and the Echo for calls and messaging, see Chapter 8.

Echo Show lights

The Echo Show does not have a light ring in the same way as the standard Echo and the Echo Dot, but it does have a colored bar at the bottom of the screen that denotes similar states to the light ring. These include:

- **Band of orange**. This is displayed when the Echo Show is ready to be set up to a Wi-Fi network, or is experiencing problems with the network.

- **Band of blue with a cyan dot.** This indicates Alexa is listening to a command after the wake word has been spoken. The cyan dot indicates the direction from where the command has come.

- **Band of red**. This indicates that the microphone has been turned off and Alexa is not in listening mode – i.e. voice commands cannot be actioned.

If calls or messages are sent to an Echo Show, these are displayed on the screen.

If the volume for an Echo device is being changed manually, the light ring pulses white – see page 22.

Changing the Volume

The volume of an Echo device can be changed in a number of ways. To do this:

Changing the volume manually

Don't forget

When the volume is being changed manually, the light ring at the top of the Echo device pulses white.

1 Press the **+** and **-** buttons on the top of the Echo device (standard Echo and Echo Dot)

Don't forget

For the Echo Show, the manual volume buttons are located along the top of the device. The volume can be changed here in the same way as for using the Alexa app.

Changing the volume with the Alexa app

The volume can be changed with the Alexa app:

1 Open the Alexa app and, when music is playing, tap on the speaker icon

Graceland • Paul Simon
Nick's Echo

Home   Communicate   Play   Devices

Don't forget

For details about playing music with the Alexa app, see Chapter 7.

2 Drag the slider or tap on either speaker icons to change the volume

Nick's Echo

or

1 Open the Alexa app and tap on the **Devices** button on the bottom toolbar

2 Tap on the **Echo & Alexa** button

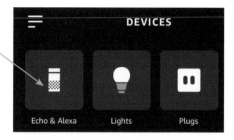

3 Tap on an Echo device

4 Drag the slider to change the volume

Tap on the **Audio Settings** button in Step 4 to access options for editing the bass, midrange and treble settings for the selected Echo device.

Changing the volume with voice commands

Voice commands can be used to change the volume of Alexa or any media that is playing – e.g. music:

- "Alexa, volume up 1"

- "Alexa, volume to 6"

- "Alexa, mute volume"

Adding More Devices

Alexa works very effectively with multiple Echo devices in the home, and also other devices such as smart lighting. These items can be added through the Alexa app, in a similar way to adding an Echo initially. To do this:

1. Open the Amazon Alexa app on a smartphone or tablet

2. Plug in the new device and tap on this button to access the **Menu**

3. Tap on the **Add Device** button and add the device in the same way as for adding the initial device

or:

1. Open the Amazon Alexa app and tap on the **Devices** button on the bottom toolbar

2. In the **Devices** section, tap on the **+** button to start adding a new device

3. Tap on the **Add Device** button to add a new device in the same way as for adding the initial device

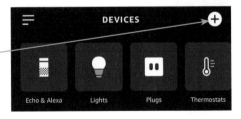

Hot tip

All of the devices that have been added via the Alexa app can be viewed by tapping on the icons in the **Devices** section.

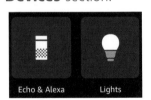

2 Uses for Alexa

Alexa can be as flexible as your imagination in terms of answering questions. This chapter looks at some of the exciting ways in which Alexa can be used.

Alexa's Built-in Skills

Alexa can have its functionality extended extensively through the use of Alexa skills (see Chapter 4). However, as soon as Alexa has been set up it is ready for use and can interact with a range of voice commands. This includes giving news updates, telling jokes, finding recipes, and translating words. To find out some of the functions that Alexa can perform:

1 Open the Alexa app

2 Tap on the **Menu** button

3 Tap on the **Things to Try** button

4 The **Things to Try** categories are listed. Some of these require additional skills to be added in order to use them, but some can be accessed with a single voice command

The items in the **Things to Try** section just give examples of commands that can be used with Alexa on an Echo device. You cannot action the commands from the examples on the **Things to Try** page.

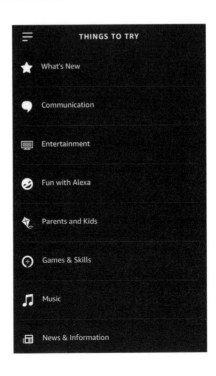

THINGS TO TRY

⭐ What's New

💬 Communication

🖥 Entertainment

😀 Fun with Alexa

🪁 Parents and Kids

⊕ Games & Skills

🎵 Music

🗞 News & Information

5 Tap on the **Fun with Alexa** button

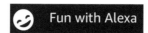

6 Tap on the **Alexa's Talents** button to view some of the entertainment options that Alexa can perform

7 The **Alexa's Talents** page lists a range of commands that can be used with Alexa to keep you entertained, such as telling jokes or singing songs

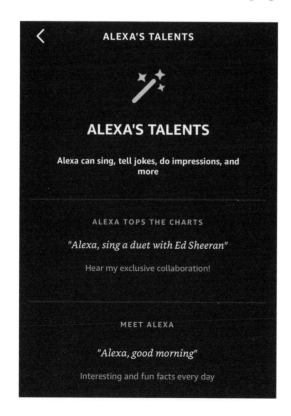

Hot tip

If you say: "Alexa, good morning", the response will include an interesting fact related to the current day. The fact is repeated if you use the command again on the same day.

...cont'd

8 Tap on the **News & Information** button in Step 4 on page 26

9 The full range of **News & Information** categories is listed. These can be used to discover the type of useful information that Alexa can convey

Alexa will make an attempt to answer even the most random questions. However, if there is something Alexa does not know, the answer will be: "Sorry, I'm not sure".

10 Tap on the **Questions & Answers** button on the News & Information page to view the type of general questions that can be asked of Alexa

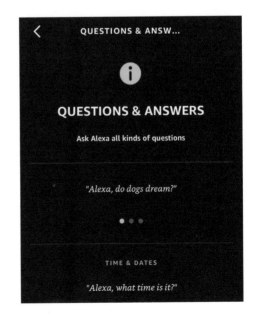

11 Tap on the **Recipes & Cooking** button on the News & Information page to view the type of cooking questions that can be asked of Alexa

12 Tap on the **Weather** button on the News & Information page to view the type of meteorological questions that can be asked of Alexa

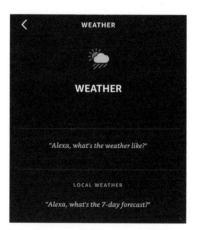

Hot tip

Alexa is an excellent option for translating foreign words and also longer phrases. The translations are provided with the appropriate accents, as applicable.

13 Tap on the **Translations** button on the News & Information page to view the type of language questions that can be asked of Alexa

Don't forget

Tap on the **Menu** button on the homepage of the Alexa app to access the available categories, including the Reminders & Alarms section.

Don't forget

Alexa on an Echo will announce reminders automatically, at the appropriate time.

Don't forget

See pages 96-106 for details about creating and working with reminders.

Being Reminded

Once the Alexa app and an Echo device have both been set up, they can be used so that Alexa can receive commands either through the app or as a voice command to the Echo. Alexa will then respond through the Echo.

One of the most effective uses for Alexa is for setting reminders for a range of tasks:

- Taking regular medication.

- Household tasks, which can be set for daily or weekly.

- Reminders for regular phone calls to family and friends.

- Shopping for essentials each week.

Once reminders have been added, either directly via the Echo device or via the Alexa app, they are displayed in the **Reminders & Alarms** section on the app.

Reminders & Alarms

Tap on a reminder to view its full details.

Getting Organized

Lists are a great way of getting organized, and Alexa is adept at creating and reciting lists. As with reminders, they can be created directly with Alexa on the Echo, or through the Alexa app. Whichever way they are created, the details can be viewed on the Alexa app in the **Lists** section. By default, the Shopping and To-do lists are already created. Subsequent lists that are created appear under the **My Lists** heading.

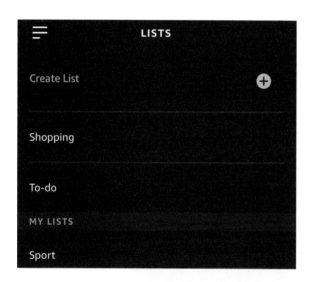

Tap on the **Create List** button to start a new list.

31

Tap on a list to view its details, and add new list items by tapping on the **Add Item** button.

Music to your Ears

Using Alexa on an Echo device is an excellent way to listen to music, and also audiobooks such as those available on Amazon. Alexa has access to the standard Amazon Music library, and commands to play music can be made directly to Alexa on the Echo or through the Alexa app.

Playing music and audiobooks through the Alexa app is done through the **Play** section. Tap on an item to play it on the Echo device.

The standard Amazon Music library offers over two million songs that can be played for free on an Echo device with Alexa. There is also a Music Unlimited option, which is a monthly subscription service that offers over 50 million songs.

See Chapter 7 for further details on playing music with Alexa and listening to audiobooks.

Swipe up the Play page to access more content and also to link to other music accounts such as Spotify and Apple Music.

Game Time

Using Alexa should be fun and there are a range of opportunities for playing games with Alexa. Some of these are already installed with Alexa, and more can also be added with a range of skills. This is similar to adding an app on a smartphone or tablet: the skill adds the functionality to Alexa so that new tasks can be performed. The skills are added using the Alexa app, and there is a specific category for **Games & Trivia**.

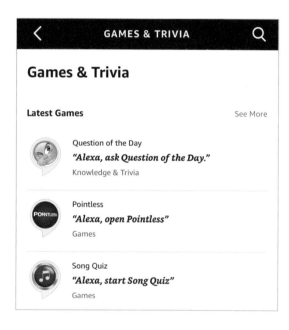

See pages 54-59 for details about accessing and adding skills for Alexa to use.

33

Once a game has been selected, tap on the **Enable to Use** button to add it to Alexa and access it via an Echo device.

Catching Up

As well as being able to provide information and entertainment, Alexa is also a good communicator. There are options for calling and messaging friends and family so that you can keep up-to-date with what's happening. This can be set up in the Alexa app, in the **Communicate** section, and after this is done calls and messages can be made, hands-free, by asking Alexa.

Don't forget

See Chapter 8 for details about communicating with people using Alexa.

Use the **Call** and **Message** buttons to perform the related task. Tap on the **Add Number** button to add the smartphone number of someone to contact.

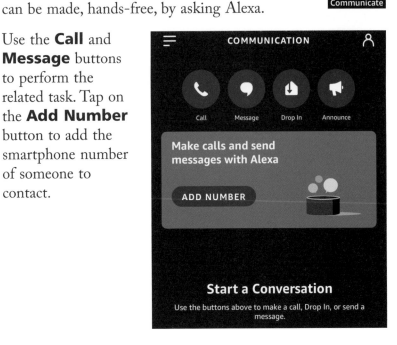

Hot tip

Once contacts have been added to the Alexa app, calls can be made to them, and messages sent to them, with Alexa and the Echo, by saying: "Alexa, call Nick".

When a new call or message is activated, the recipient can be selected from your contacts.

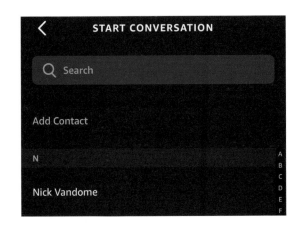

Keeping in Touch

Alexa is also adept at communicating within the home, using other Alexa-enabled devices, and also for making short announcements. These are done with the **Drop In** and **Announce** features, both of which are available in the **Communicate** section of the Alexa app.

Announcements can be made via the Alexa app, wherever you are, and will be played by Alexa on the selected device.

> ### ANNOUNCEMENT
>
> I'm nearly home
>
> →

Don't forget

See pages 142-143 for details about using the **Drop In** and **Announce** features with Alexa.

35

The Drop In feature can be used to call another Echo device, either from the Alexa app, or hands-free from an Echo device.

Controlling a Smart Home

Alexa can be used to control a range of devices, not just Echo devices. It is an excellent way to control smart home devices such as lighting and heating. Once the required skills have been added to Alexa, it is possible to control and manage smart home devices with voice controls. Smart home devices can be added in the **Devices** section of the Alexa app.

Items that have been added can be viewed from the related buttons in the **Devices** section.

Don't forget

See Chapter 10 for details about using Alexa with smart home devices.

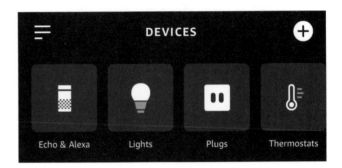

Tap on an item to view the elements that are linked to it. The elements can then be turned on or off as required. This can also be done with voice commands using Alexa on an Echo device.

3 Using the Alexa App

A lot of the functionality for Alexa is controlled through the Alexa app. This chapter shows how to access and use the app.

Around the Alexa App

The Alexa app serves to add further functionality to Alexa, so that more voice commands can be actioned on an Echo device. It is also possible to action a range of commands via the app itself. To get started with the app:

1 Open the Alexa app and tap on the **Home** button at the bottom of the screen to view the homepage

Home

Don't forget

The location in Step 2 is the location of the smartphone or tablet on which the Alexa app has been downloaded. The Echo device can have a different location, and this can be specified within the Alexa app's settings. See page 48 for details about how to set the location for an Echo device.

2 The top panel displays the day and date, and also weather conditions for your location (this can be set when the Alexa app is first set up, and it can also be amended through the app's settings; see page 48 for details)

3 Tap on the **Communicate** button at the bottom of the screen to access options for calling or messaging people, or communicating with Echo devices

Communicate

4 Tap on this button at the bottom of the screen to access options to enable communication between the app and Alexa

5 Tap on the **Allow** button to give Alexa permission to access the microphone on your smartphone or tablet, and also access your location. This will enable you to communicate with Alexa via your smartphone or tablet

Talk to Alexa with your app

To get started, give Alexa permission to access your microphone and location to do the following and more:

• Allow Alexa to hear your requests
• Call and message friends and family
• Control Smart Home devices
• Get location relevant search results, traffic and weather

LATER   ALLOW

Don't forget

Once Alexa has been given permission to access the microphone on your smartphone or tablet, and access its location, voice commands can be made to Alexa by tapping the button in Step 4.

6 Tap on the **Play** button at the bottom of the screen (see screenshot in Step 2) to access audio options

Play

MUSIC & BOOKS

RECENTLY PLAYED

Classic Rock
Amazon Music

Radio 2
TuneIn

AMAZON MUSIC   Open App

Classic Rock   Fleetwood Mac   Queen

Around the Homepage

Once the Alexa app has been downloaded and set up, the homepage can be used to view information related to your location, and view panels for suggested uses for Alexa. To view the homepage of the Alexa app:

1 Open the Alexa app and tap on the **Home** button at the bottom of the screen to view the homepage

Alexa uses your location for a range of important tasks, such as providing local weather forecasts and travel directions.

2 The top panel displays information about your current location. Tap on the **Set Your Location** button to give Alexa access to your current location

Wednesday, February 26

PERTH
AccuWeather.com

Morning · Afternoon · Evening
5° · 5° · 0°

Set Your Location

"I'm on my way"
Send an announcement from your phone to Echo devices in your home.

3 Below the top panel are cards with suggested uses for Alexa

4 Any media that is currently playing (e.g. music or a radio station) is displayed above the bottom toolbar

5 Swipe up the homepage to view all of the cards.
Tap on the **Try Now** button to see the functionality of a suggested card

"I'm on my way"

Send an announcement from your phone to Echo devices in your home.

TRY NOW

Hot tip

Latest trending news cards also appear on the homepage.

6 To remove a card from the homepage, tap here on the card and tap on the **Dismiss** button

TRY SAYING

"Alexa, sing happy birthday"

Tap to explore more

Dismiss

Alexa App Settings

Within the Alexa app is a range of settings for both the Alexa and the Echo. These can be used to set up Alexa and the Echo to operate exactly how you want them. To access the settings on the Alexa app:

1 Open the Alexa app and tap on the **Menu** button

2 Tap on the **Settings** button

3 The full list of settings categories is displayed. Tap on one of the categories to view its options

It is worth taking some time to get to know all of the settings on the Alexa app as this will make it quicker to change any options when you need to.

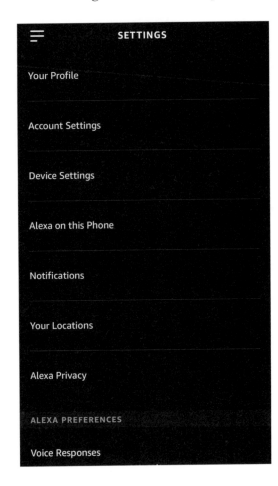

SETTINGS

Your Profile

Account Settings

Device Settings

Alexa on this Phone

Notifications

Your Locations

Alexa Privacy

ALEXA PREFERENCES

Voice Responses

Profile settings

These can be used to add your own details that can be used by Alexa. To do this:

1 Tap on the **Your Profile** button   Your Profile

2 Tap on the **Edit Name** button to change the name used by Alexa

Tap on the **Add** button next to the **Mobile Number** option in Step 2 to add a smartphone number so that you can make hands-free calls and send messages directly from Alexa, using voice controls.

43

3 Tap on the **Create** button next to the **Voice** option to create a voice profile. This helps Alexa learn your specific voice, call you by your name, and personalize the whole Alexa experience. Tap on the **Consent** button to set up the voice profile

After the **Consent** button has been tapped in Step 3 there is a step-by-step process for setting up the voice profile, for use with Alexa on an Echo device. Start by saying: **"Alexa, recognize my voice"** and then repeat four phrases provided by Alexa. After this, the voice profile is done.

...cont'd

Account settings

These can be used to apply settings for the user's account:

Don't forget

Another option within the Account settings is to view details about Amazon Household members. This is people who have been set up to share content that has been bought from Amazon, such as apps or Prime Video. People can be added to Amazon Household from your Amazon account on the Amazon website.

1 Tap on the **Account Settings** button

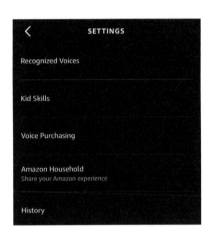

2 The Account settings include identifying someone's voice, adding skills specifically for children, authorizing voice purchasing with Alexa, and viewing the history of voice commands

Device settings

These can be used to apply settings for specific devices:

1 Tap on the **Device Settings** button

2 Tap on a device to access its specific settings

3 Each device can have its own settings applied

4 Tap on an **Echo** device in Step 2 under **Device Settings** on the previous page to apply its specific settings. This can include the volume for the device, and its connected Wi-Fi network. Tap on the **Change** button to connect to a different Wi-Fi network

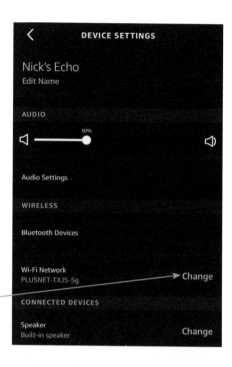

Specific device settings for setting or changing the location of the Echo device and changing the wake word are shown on pages 48 and 49 respectively.

5 Tap on the **Alexa on this Phone** option in Step 2 under **Device Settings** on the previous page to apply its specific settings. These will be different from those applied for any Echo device

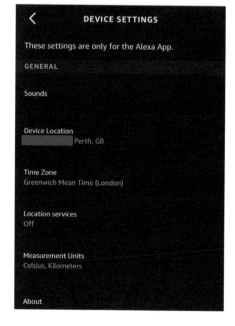

If **Location services** are **Off** for the Alexa app on a smartphone, tap on it to turn it **On**. This will enable the app to recognize your location wherever you are.

...cont'd

Alexa on this Phone settings

These can be used to apply settings for the Alexa app on a smartphone or tablet:

1 Tap on the **Alexa on this Phone** button

Alexa on this Phone

2 Apply settings for the Alexa app on the device, as in Step 5 on page 45

Notifications settings

These can be used to specify how Alexa notifies you about certain items. To apply these:

Hot tip

The Amazon Shopping option in Step 2 for the Notifications settings can be used to notify you when items that have been ordered from Amazon are out for delivery.

1 Tap on the **Notifications** button

Notifications

2 Tap on a notification item (e.g. **Reminders**) to select how Alexa deals with notifications

NOTIFICATIONS

Reminders
Disabled

Amazon Shopping

Things To Try

3 Notifications have to be turned **On** in the Settings section of the device on which Alexa is installed. Tap on the **Notifications** button and drag the **Allow Notifications** button **On**

‹ Settings   **Amazon Alexa**

ALLOW AMAZON ALEXA TO ACCESS

✈ Location   Always ›

📷 Notifications   ›
Off

‹ Back   **Notifications**

Allow Notifications

Your Locations settings

These can be used to assign specific addresses for different locations (e.g. home or work) or a customized location:

1 Tap on the **Your Locations** button

2 Tap on an address (e.g. **Home Address**) to add an address that can be used by Alexa

Hot tip

Tap on the **Add Location** button in Step 2 for the **Your Locations** settings to add an address for another family member. This can then be used to enter commands for this address – e.g.: "Alexa, give me the weather forecast when I get to Emily's house".

Alexa Privacy settings

These can be used to view and control privacy information related to using Alexa and the data that is generated:

1 Tap on the **Alexa Privacy** button

2 Tap on one of the Alexa Privacy topics to view information about it – e.g. tap on the **Manage Your Alexa Data** topic to see details about how data created on Alexa is used, including being able to delete voice recordings that have been made

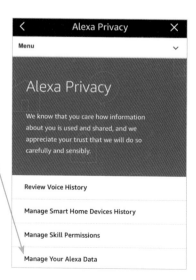

Location services have to be turned **On**, for your smartphone or tablet and the Alexa app, for the Your Locations settings to work effectively.

47

Setting your Location

It is important that Alexa knows your location (or more accurately, the location of your Amazon Echo) so that specific items can be tailored to it – i.e. when you ask for the current weather, or restaurant recommendations nearby. To set the location of your Echo with the Alexa app's settings:

Don't forget

Alexa uses your location for a range of important tasks, including travel directions.

1 Open the Alexa app and access **Menu > Settings > Device Settings**

Device Settings

2 Select an Echo device

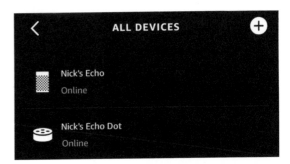

3 Swipe up the page and tap on the **Device Location** option

Device Location
10 Seaview, Perth, GB

4 Edit the location as required and tap on the **Save** button

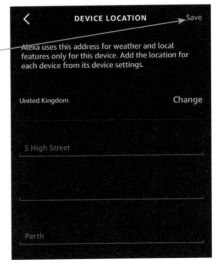

5 The location entered in Step 4 is displayed under the **Device Location** heading, and this will be used by Alexa

Changing the Wake Word

By default, the wake word for the Alexa is "Alexa". This is what must be said before the device will become active and responsive to your commands. However, this can be changed in the Alexa app. To do this:

1 Open the Alexa app and access **Menu > Settings > Device Settings**

> Device Settings

2 Tap on the **Wake Word** button

> Wake Word
> Alexa

3 Tap on a word to make it the new wake word

Beware

Different wake words can be used on separate Echo devices. However, it is best to keep the same wake word for all of the Echo devices that you have, to avoid confusion.

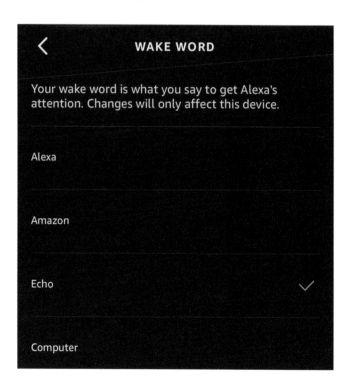

WAKE WORD

Your wake word is what you say to get Alexa's attention. Changes will only affect this device.

Alexa

Amazon

Echo ✓

Computer

4 The new wake word is displayed on the Device Settings page

Checking Voice Commands

When using voice commands it is important to know that Alexa has understood you correctly. This can be checked from within the Alexa app. To do this:

1 Open the Alexa app and tap on the **Home** button at the bottom of the screen to view the homepage

2 Tap on this button at the top of the window to access the Alexa app main menu

3 Tap on the **Activity** button on the main menu

4 The most recent voice requests are shown at the top of the Activity page

Not all voice requests appear on the Activity page. Simple ones, such as "Alexa, what is the time?", do not appear.

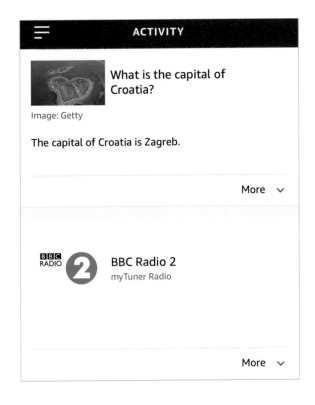

5 Tap on the **More** button next to a voice request to view details about it in the **Voice feedback** section

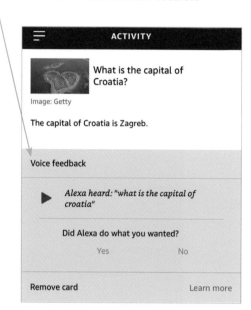

6 Tap on the **Yes** or **No** buttons to provide feedback about whether Alexa heard your command correctly and acted accordingly. This is used to train Alexa for subsequent requests

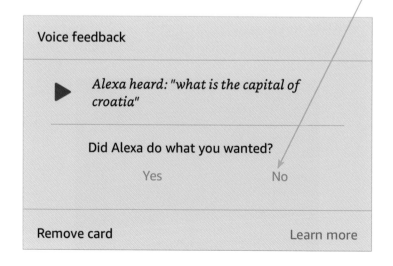

Tap on the **Learn more** button in Step 6 to view **Help & Feedback** topics for Alexa and its devices.

Alexa Preferences

In addition to the Alexa app settings for Echo devices and your own details, there are also preferences for Alexa itself. These can be used to specify options for Alexa and how it communicates with you. To use these preferences:

Don't forget

The Alexa preferences will be noted throughout the book as required – e.g. for setting up a Flash Briefing for a daily news update.

1 Open the Alexa app and access the Settings section, as shown on page 42. Tap on one of the categories to view its options

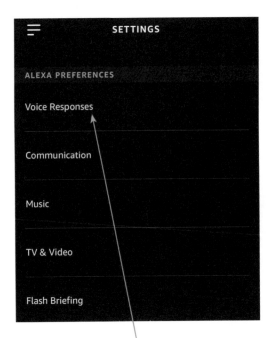

2 Tap on the **Voice Responses** option in Step 1 and drag the **Brief Mode** button **On** to enable Alexa to just play a sound when a command has been completed, rather than speak a reply

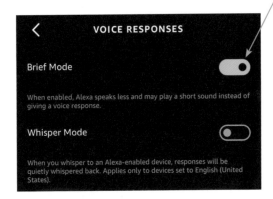

4 Adding Alexa Skills

The operation of Alexa can be expanded by adding skills with the Alexa app. This chapter shows how to do this.

Accessing Skills

The tasks that Alexa can perform are known as skills. This is similar to using an app on a smartphone or a tablet. Some skills are already built in for Alexa, while others can be added to increase Alexa's functionality. For instance, providing the time and date is a built-in skill, while managing a calendar is a skill that can be added. To access the available skills for Alexa:

Beware

Skills cannot be added directly with Alexa on an Echo device; they have to be added using the Alexa app.

54

1 Open the Alexa app

2 Tap on the **Menu** button

3 Tap on the **Skills & Games** button

Skills & Games

4 Tap on the **Discover** tab

Discover

5 The Skills & Games page is displayed. The top panel contains featured skills, with individual skills listed below

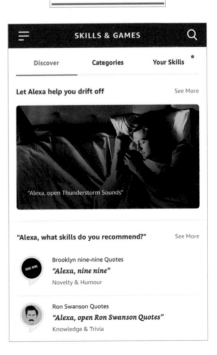

6 Swipe up and down the page to view all of the available recommended skills

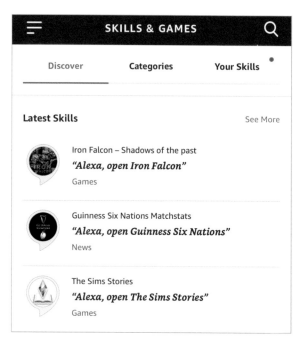

The skills under the **Latest Skills** heading on the **Discover** page change on a regular basis, as more skills are added for Alexa to use.

7 Tap on a specific skill to view its details. Tap on the **Enable To Use** button to add the skill to Alexa so that it can be accessed using voice commands

Once a skill has been added it is usually activated on Alexa by naming the skill – e.g. "Alexa, ask myTuner Radio Player to play pop music".

...cont'd

8 Tap on the **Categories** tab at the top of the window

Categories

9 The full range of categories of skills is displayed, with featured categories at the top of the window

The icons under the **Featured Categories** heading at the top of the **Skills & Games** window contain the same content as accessing the category from the **All Categories** list.

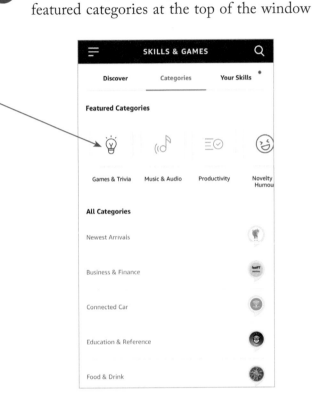

10 Swipe up the window to view the full range of categories that can be used to add skills to Alexa

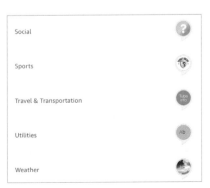

56

11 Tap on a category to view the skills within it. Tap on a skill to view its details

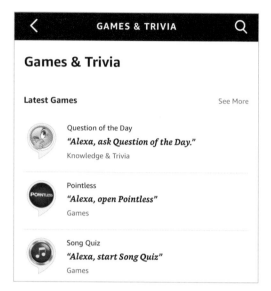

Examples of using skills are all given using "Alexa" as the wake word. If you have changed the wake word, then this should be used instead. For details about changing the wake word, see page 49.

57

12 Tap on the **Search** icon at the top of the Skills & Games window to search for specific topics

13 Enter a keyword or skill name in the Search box. Matching topics are shown below the search word, and matching skills are shown below this

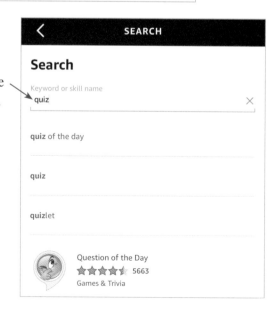

Adding Skills

Numerous skills can be added for Alexa, to increase the overall functionality of the system. To do this:

1 Open the Alexa app

2 Tap on the **Menu** button

3 Tap on the **Skills & Games** button

Skills & Games

4 Tap on a skill in the **Discover** window, or search for one using the **Categories** tab or the **Search** icon at the top of the window

Hot tip

Skills can be removed using the Alexa app, so it is worth trying as many as you like: you can always remove the ones you do not want once you have tested them all.

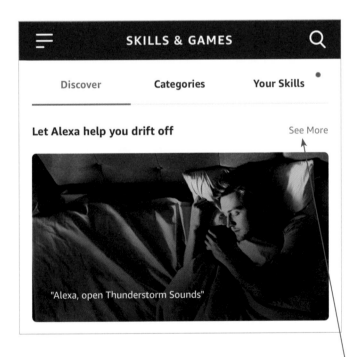

5 Tap on a skill to view its details or, on the Discover page, tap on the **See More** button

6 Details of the skill are displayed

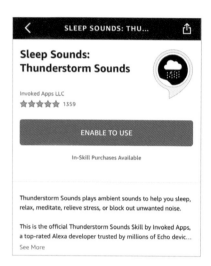

If a skill states that there are **In-Skill Purchases Available**, this means that there is additional functionality for the skill, but this will have to be paid for.

7 Swipe up the page to view more details about the skill, including phrases that can be used with it

8 Tap on the **Enable to Use** button in Step 6 to add the

ENABLE TO USE

skill to Alexa. It will also be available to view in the **Your Skills** section, see pages 60-61

Managing your Skills

Once a new skill has been enabled it will be available for Alexa on a compatible Echo device. It is possible to view all of the skills that you have added to Alexa and manage them as required. To do this:

1 Open the Alexa app and access **Menu** > **Skills & Games** as shown on page 58

2 Tap on the **Your Skills** tab in the top right-hand corner of the Skills & Games window

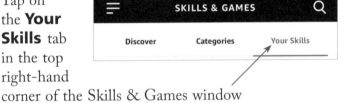

3 The **Your Skills** page is where you can manage the skills used by Alexa. Tap on the **Enabled** button to view all of the skills that have been added

Tap here on the Your Skills page to display the skills on the page in **Alphabetical** order or by the most **Recent** item added. Tap on the **Done** button after a selection has been made.

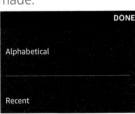

4 Tap on the **Updated** button to view all of the skills that have been updated since they were first enabled (swipe along the panel below the **Your Skills** tab to view each option)

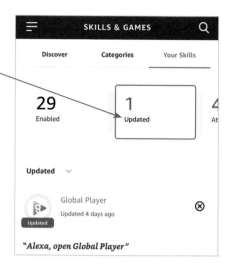

If there is a green dot next to the **Your Skills** tab, this means that a skill has recently been updated. Tap on the **Updated** button to view the details.

5 Tap on the **Attention** button to view skills that require an action to be taken, such as linking them to an online account

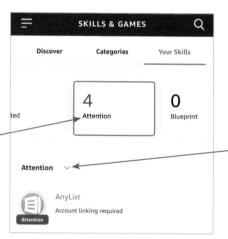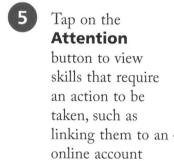

Tap here to access a shortcut menu to the other pages on the **Your Skills** section. Tap on an item and tap on the **Done** button to move to that page.

6 Tap on the **Blueprint** button to start creating customized skills, based on templates provided by the Alexa app or the Amazon website (see pages 62-69 for details)

Creating Skills with Blueprints

Within the Skills & Games section of the Alexa app it is possible to create your own skills by selecting templates and customizing the content to your own requirements. These are known as Blueprints, and the templates to be customized can be accessed from the Alexa app and also from the Amazon website. Once a skill has been created with Blueprints it is available with Alexa on an Echo device, and it will also be visible in the Your Skills section of the Alexa app.

Blueprints in the Alexa app

To create your own skills using the Alexa app:

Don't forget

Once a new skill has been created using a Blueprint template, it will be listed under the **Blueprint** button in Step 2.

1 Open the Alexa app and access the **Your Skills** section as shown on page 60

2 Tap on the **Blueprint** button

3 Tap on the **Create More Skills** button to access the Blueprint templates, from which customized skills can be created

4 Tap on the **Discover** tab to view the available Blueprint templates and their categories. The **Discover** page opens at the **Featured** section, with the latest Blueprints

Tap on the **Your Skills** tab in Step 4 to access information about your Amazon account. This has to be confirmed before Blueprint templates can be used. Check your account details and change them, if required. After changes are made, or if no changes are needed, tap on the **Update Account** button.

UPDATE ACCOUNT

5 Swipe along this bar to view the different categories. Tap on a category to view its options

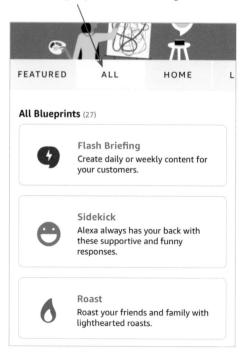

...cont'd

6 Tap on one of the main category headings and tap on a Blueprint to view its details

7 Review the details of the Blueprint and tap on the **Make Your Own** button at the bottom of the page to create a skill using this Blueprint

MAKE YOUR OWN

Hot tip

Tap on the **Play** button in Step 7 to hear a preview of the Blueprint as it will appear once a skill has been created from it.

...cont'd

8 The default content is shown for the Blueprint

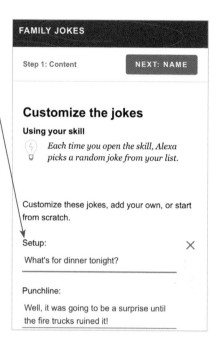

9 Enter customized content instead of the default content, and tap on the **Next: Name** button

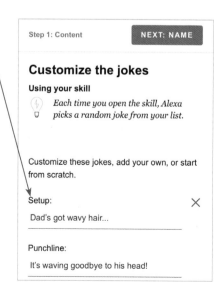

If there are multiple items in a Blueprint skill, Alexa will pick them at random when the skill is accessed – e.g. jokes will be selected in any order.

10 The Blueprint has a default name that can be used for the skill, if required

The name of the Blueprint, whether it is left as the default one or changed, is the one that is used to access the skill on Alexa once it has been created.

11 To change the default name, tap on it and enter new text that will be used as the skill's name

12 Tap on the **Next: Create Skill** button in Step 10 to create the skill

...cont'd

13 A confirmation page appears once the skill has been created

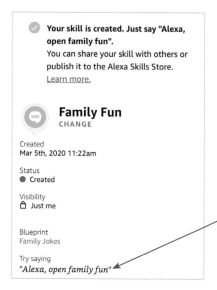

The confirmation page in Step 13 contains the command that can be used to access the skill – e.g. "Alexa, open family fun".

14 In the **Your Skills** section of the Alexa app, the new skill is listed under the **Blueprint** section

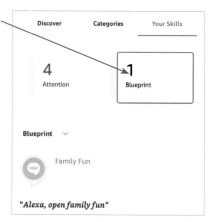

15 The new skill is also displayed in the **Enabled** section

...cont'd

Blueprints on the Amazon website

It is also possible to create skills from Blueprints from the Amazon website, using a desktop computer or a laptop. To do this:

You need to sign in to your Amazon account before you access the Blueprints, so that any skills that you create here are available with Alexa on an Echo device.

1 Open the Amazon Blueprints page at **https://blueprints.amazon.com** (or **.co.uk**)

2 Click on the **Sign In** button to sign in to your Amazon account

3 Enter the sign-in details for your Amazon account and click on the **Sign-In** button

4 Scroll up the page to view the categories for the Blueprints, and the individual items that can be used to create new skills

5 Click on a Blueprint to view its details, and click on the **Make Your Own** button to start creating a customized skill from the Blueprint

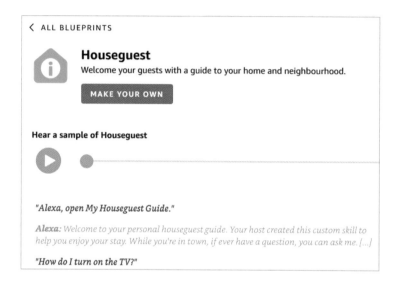

Don't forget

Once a new skill has been created from a Blueprint on the Amazon website it will be visible in the **Your Skills** section of the Alexa app, under the **Enabled** and **Blueprint** buttons.

6 Enter the customized details into the Blueprint template to create your own skill. Click on the **Next** buttons to move through the process to create the final skill

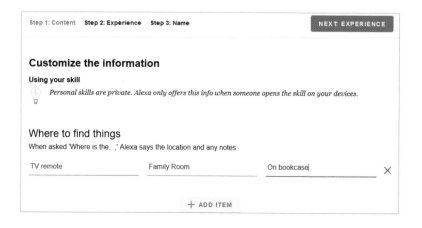

Beware

Once a new skill has been created from a Blueprint it can be accessed by asking Alexa a question, preceded by the name of the skill – e.g. "Alexa, ask My Questions, What's happening". If the name of the skill is not used, Alexa may give a different response.

Using Skills

Because of the range of skills available for Alexa, there is no definitive way to use them. However, a good starting point can be to ask Alexa about a specific skill. For instance, if you are using the Sleep Sounds skill you can ask Alexa for details about it, such as:

- "Alexa, tell me about Sleep Sounds"

Details about a skill can also be viewed on the Activity page of the Alexa app. For instance, you can ask Alexa to list the sounds within the Sleep Sounds skill, and these will be listed within the Alexa app too – e.g.:

- "Alexa, list the Sleep Sounds"

Don't forget

Some details about skills and commands that have been made can be viewed on the **Activity** page within the Alexa app.

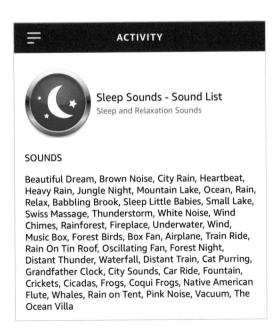

When using a skill it is sometimes necessary to ask Alexa to access the skill and then request an item within it – e.g.:

- "Alexa, ask Sleep Sounds to play Heartbeat"

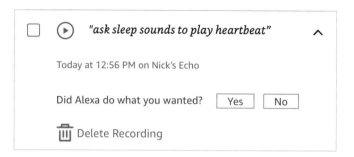

- If the skill name is not mentioned (e.g. "Alexa, play heartbeat"), another item may be accessed by Alexa, such as a song by the same name.

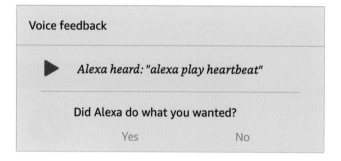

Hot tip

On the **Activity** page within the Alexa app, if an item has a **Read More** button next to it, this means that there is more information about the item, usually on a web page, that can be accessed from the button.

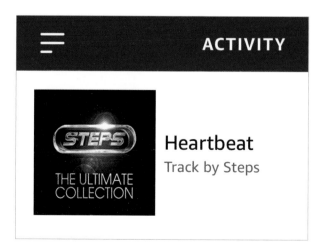

Disabling Skills

Skills can be disabled from use, so that they are not available to Alexa. However, this does not delete them completely, and they can be enabled again if required. To disable a skill:

1 Open the Alexa app and access the **Your Skills** section as shown on page 54

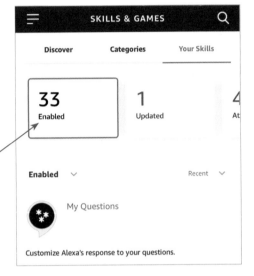

2 Under the **Enabled** section, tap on a skill

Hot tip

Once a skill has been disabled it can be enabled again by searching for it, as shown on page 55, and tapping on the **Enable To Use** button.

3 Tap on the **Disable Skill** button

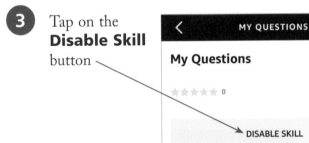

4 Tap on the **Disable** button to confirm the action

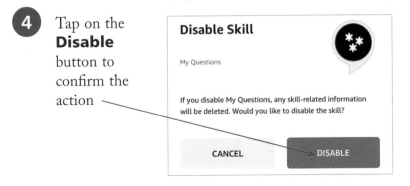

72

5 Questioning Alexa

This chapter looks at the range of questions that can be used with Alexa, including getting the news and traffic details.

Questions to Ask

Once the Echo and Alexa have been set up you can start making requests of Alexa. Each request has to begin with "Alexa…" (or the wake word you have chosen), otherwise you will be met with a stony silence. Some simple questions to ask Alexa to begin with include:

- "Alexa, what time is it?"

- "Alexa, what is the current weather?" (This is based on the location of the Echo, as shown on page 48.)

- "Alexa, will it rain tomorrow?"

- "Alexa, play radio station XXX" (Alexa will play the requested radio station as long as it is available on TuneIn, which is the radio player for the Echo and Alexa.)

- "Alexa, play [selected music or artist]" (This is taken from any music that you have in your Amazon Music library, which has either been bought from Amazon or streamed from a streaming service.)

- "Alexa, stop"

- "Alexa, pause"

- "Alexa, volume up/down" or "Alexa, volume [1-10]"

- "Alexa, tell me a joke"

- "Alexa, set a timer for XX minutes"

- "Alexa, what is the definition of [selected word]?"

Don't forget

See Chapter 7 for more details about using Alexa to play music and radio stations.

74

≡   **ACTIVITY**

What is the definition of loquacious?

The adjective 'loquacious' is usually defined as: talking or tending to talk much or freely; talkative; chattering; babbling; garrulous. For more, ask me to give you more definitions for 'loquacious'.

- "Alexa, tell me the news" (This can be customized with different news providers; see pages 76-79 for details.)

- "Alexa how do you say [selected word] in [selected language]?"

- "Alexa, what is the square root of 81?"

- "Alexa, what is the capital of [country]?"

- "Alexa, what movies are playing nearby?" (This is based on the location for the Echo, as shown on page 48.)

In theaters near you

Popular movies Monday, 9 March:

Onward
IMDb: **7.7**/10

Military Wives
IMDb: **6.7**/10

The Invisible...
IMDb: **7.5**/10

If you ask Alexa a question such as "Alexa, what is the best movie of all time?", the answer will be based on information from the web, such as movie details from IMDb, the online movie database.

- "Alexa, list Italian restaurants nearby"

- "Alexa, help" to get details of the type of help questions that can be asked – e.g. "Alexa, how do I connect to Bluetooth?"

- "Alexa, how many kilometers in a mile?"

- "Alexa, how many grams in an ounce?"

- "Alexa, how many US dollars to the UK pound?"

- "Alexa, give me a recipe for [selected dish]"

- "Alexa, give me a tip"

Getting the News

Alexa is an excellent option for keeping up with the daily news, and you can request a news update at any time, simply by saying: "Alexa, what's the news?". This will result in a news briefing that is taken from specific online news services. This is known as a Flash Briefing, and it is possible to customize this so that your news comes from one or more of your favorite news outlets. To do this:

The Flash Briefing can also be activated by saying: "Alexa, what's my Flash Briefing?".

1 Open the Alexa app

2 Tap on the **Menu** button

3 Tap on the **Settings** button **Settings**

4 Under the **Alexa Preferences** heading tap on the **Flash Briefing** button

Flash Briefing

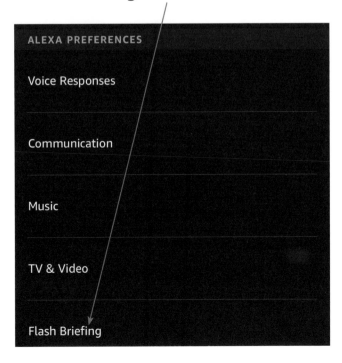

ALEXA PREFERENCES

Voice Responses

Communication

Music

TV & Video

Flash Briefing

5 On the **Flash Briefing** page, tap on the **Add Content** button to add the news service providers for the items in the Flash Briefing

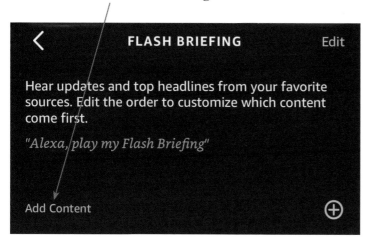

6 The items that can be used with the Flash Briefing are displayed. Tap on an item to view its details

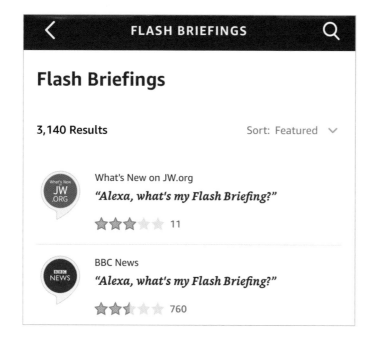

If you stop a Flash Briefing before it has been completed, you can access it again and only the unheard stories will be delivered – i.e. Alexa will not return to the beginning of the Flash Briefing.

...cont'd

7 Review the details of the item, and if you want to include it in the Flash Briefing, tap on the **Enable To Use** button

ENABLE TO USE

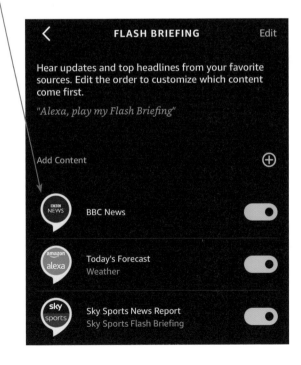

8 Repeat the process for all of the items that you want to include in the Flash Briefing. The active items are shown at the top of the window

Hot tip

If you just want to hear an update from a specific skill, rather than have it in a complete Flash Briefing, say: "Alexa, play [news item]".

Changing the Flash Briefing order

The items in the Flash Briefing are actioned by Alexa in the order in which they are listed in Step 8 on the previous page. However, it is possible to change this order, so the items are delivered in the order you want. To do this:

1 Tap on the **Edit** button in the top right-hand corner of the Flash Briefing page

2 The current order of the Flash Briefing items is displayed. This is the order in which Alexa will action the Flash Briefing items

Tap on the **Done** button in the top right-hand corner of the Edit window to confirm the reordering of the Flash Briefing.

3 Press and hold on the button to the right of an item and drag it into a new position to reorder the Flash Briefing

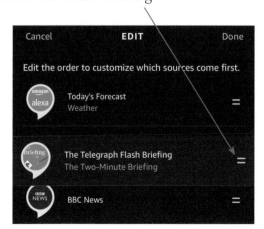

Beating the Traffic

Alexa can be used to provide traffic information between two points, so that you can plan your journey accordingly. Once the two locations have been set, Alexa will use this for the default traffic directions, until the locations are changed.

1 Open the Alexa app and access the **Settings** as shown on page 76

2 Under the **Alexa Preferences** heading tap on the **Traffic** button

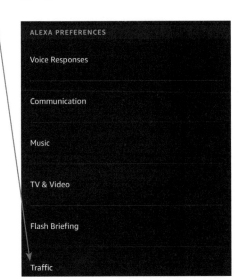

ALEXA PREFERENCES

Voice Responses

Communication

Music

TV & Video

Flash Briefing

Traffic

It is best to include two locations that you use regularly for the options in the Traffic settings – e.g. your home address and that of a family member. The locations can be changed as required, but if it is a regular route that you use, you will be able to get the traffic details each time you ask Alexa.

3 Tap on the **From** option to enter the start destination, from which the traffic information will be taken

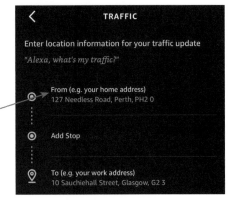

TRAFFIC

Enter location information for your traffic update

"Alexa, what's my traffic?"

From (e.g. your home address)
127 Needless Road, Perth, PH2 0

Add Stop

To (e.g. your work address)
10 Sauchiehall Street, Glasgow, G2 3

4 Enter an address for the **From** destination and tap on the **Save** button

5 Tap on the **To** option and add an address in the same way as for the **From** destination

Hot tip

Tap on the **Add Stop** button in Step 5 to add a location along the route at which you regularly stop, such as a cafe or a restaurant where you stop for lunch on the way to your destination.

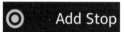

6 When you ask Alexa "Alexa, what's the traffic?", the reply will include traffic information between the two locations in the Traffic settings, and also the fastest route to take. Access the Alexa app to view details of the route, although this does not have step-by-step instructions

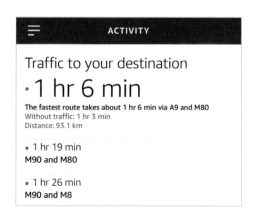

Being a Good Sport

Delivering the latest sports news is another speciality of Alexa, and it is possible to customize this for your favorite sports teams. To do this:

1 Open the Alexa app and access the **Settings** as shown on page 76

2 Under the **Alexa Preferences** heading tap on the **Sports** button

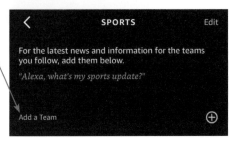

Only teams can be added to the sports news update, not individual sports people. However, requests can be made to Alexa regarding the results of individuals.

3 Tap on the **Add a Team** button to add a team, or teams, to the list that will be used by Alexa for sports news updates

4 Enter the name of a team in the Search box. Tap on one or more of the search results to select it

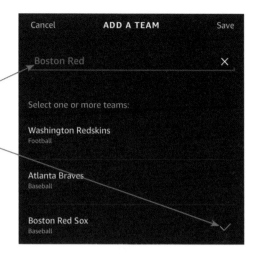

5 Tap on the **Save** button to add the selected team

6 The team is added to the list of items used in the sports update. Results from the included teams will be covered when you ask: "Alexa, what's the sports news?"

When a sports update is read out by Alexa, it includes the teams' latest results and their next fixture.

7 To remove a team, tap on the **Edit** button in Step 6, then tap here next to a team and tap on the **Save** button

One-command Routines

Alexa does not just respond to individual requests: it is also possible to create a series of commands as a sequence, and action them with a single trigger word or phrase, to which Alexa will respond with the whole sequence of commands. This is known as a routine, and is an excellent option if you regularly perform the same sequence of events – e.g. listen to the news, get the latest traffic update, and the current weather.

There are some featured routines that can be used with Alexa, and you can also create your own custom ones.

Using featured routines
To use the built-in, featured routines:

Don't forget

Built-in routines can be edited and have more elements added to them, in the same way as for creating a new routine – see pages 88-93.

1 Open the Alexa app and tap on the **Menu** button

2 Tap on the **Routines** button **Routines**

3 Tap on the **Featured** tab

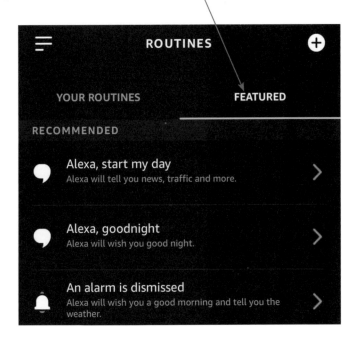

4 The details of the routine are displayed. These include whether is it disabled or enabled, its name, the trigger word or phrase (When You Say), and the actions that make up the routine

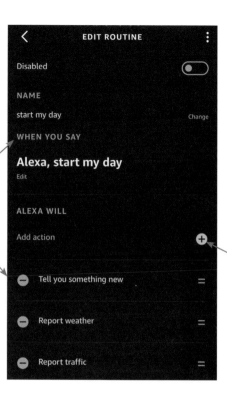

Tap on this button to add new actions to a built-in routine. See pages 90-91 for details about adding actions to a routine.

5 Tap this button **On** so that the routine is enabled

Once a routine has been enabled, it is not available below the **Recommended** heading in Step 3 on the previous page. Instead, it is available from the **Your Routines** tab. Only enabled routines can be actioned by Alexa.

6 Drag on the button next to an item to change its order in the routine

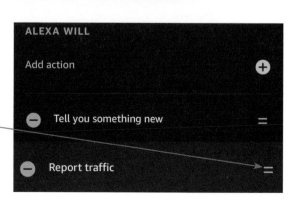

...cont'd

7 Tap on the **Change** button under the **Name** section to change the name of the routine

8 Type a new name for the routine and tap on the **Next** button

The name of a routine is what appears as its description in the Alexa app. The trigger word or phrase (When You Say) is the command used to activate the routine with Alexa on an Echo device.

9 Tap on the **Edit** button under the **When You Say** section to change the trigger word or phrase

10 Type a new trigger word or phrase for the routine, and tap on the **Next** button

11 The changes made on the previous page are displayed on the main **Edit Routine** page

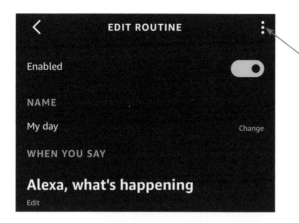

12 Swipe down to the bottom of the **Edit Routine** page and tap here to select a location from where the routine is delivered

13 Tap on a device to deliver the routine. This can include specific devices or **The device you speak to** or **This Device** – i.e. the one being used

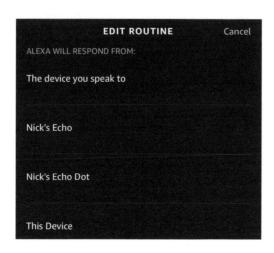

...cont'd

Creating new routines

To create your own customized routines:

1 Access the **Routines** section in the Alexa app, as shown on page 84

A routine name can be 50 characters long (including spaces).

2 Tap on the **Your Routines** tab

YOUR ROUTINES

3 Tap on the **+** button in the top right-hand corner to start creating a new routine

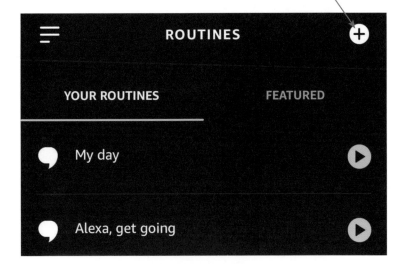

4 Tap on the **Enter routine name** option

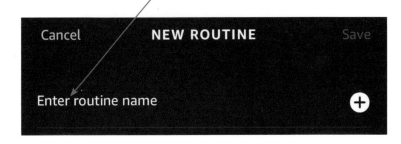

5 Enter a name for the routine and tap on the **Next** button

6 Tap on the **When this happens** button to select a trigger word or phrase for the routine

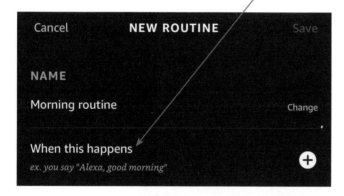

7 Tap on an option for creating a trigger for an action. This includes a voice command, a specific time, an action for a smart home device, and an action for when an alarm is dismissed

Only one trigger can be used for each routine. For instance, if the **Voice** option is selected in Step 7, a single voice command will be used to activate the routine: you cannot have a voice command and a calendar item (Schedule) as triggers for the same routine.

...cont'd

8 For the option selected in Step 7 on page 89, enter the relevant information, such as a phrase that triggers an action, and tap on the **Next** button

9 The trigger for the action is included on the **New Routine** page

Don't forget

Tap on the **Edit** button below a trigger to change it. However, this can only be used to change the trigger for the selected category. For instance, if the trigger is a **Voice** command, it cannot be edited to be another type of command, such as **Schedule**.

10 Tap on the **Add action** button to specify what happens when the trigger is used

11 Tap on one of the options for the first action of the routine. These include options for Alexa speaking a phrase, reading a calendar, making a call, sending a message, playing music, reading a Flash Briefing (News), giving a traffic update, or giving a weather forecast

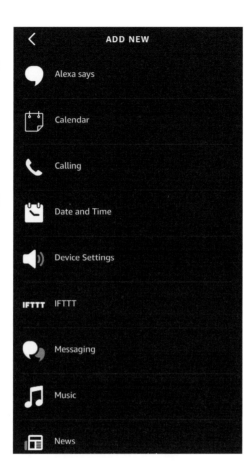

Swipe up the page in Step 11 to view the full range of items that can be included in the routine. Items such as Traffic and Weather are toward the bottom of the page.

12 The selected item is displayed in the **Confirm** window. Tap on the **Next** button to include it in the routine

...cont'd

Hot tip

The **Customized** option in Step 13 can be used to create your own response for Alexa when the trigger word or phrase is used. For instance, you could create a response so that Alexa replies: "Hello Nick, how are you today?".

13 For the **Alexa Says** option, Alexa can be asked to deliver a range of responses, including customized ones, when the trigger word or phrase is used. In addition, Alexa can also respond with a song, a joke or a story when the trigger word or phrase is used

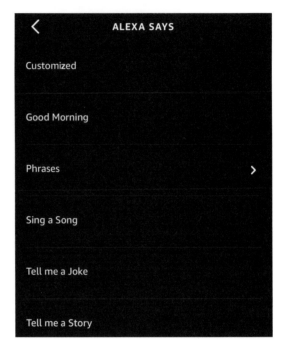

14 For the **Calendar** option, Alexa can deliver calendar events, such as today's or tomorrow's calendar, or the next event

15 For the **Music** option, Alexa can play a specific song, or songs from a specific artist, or a playlist. Click on the **Select Provider** button to select where the music is played from – e.g. Amazon Music

16 Once the items for the routine have been included, they are displayed on the **New Routine** page. Tap on the **Save** button to include the routine in the **Your Routines** section as shown on page 88

A large number of actions can be added to a routine. However, it is best not to have too many otherwise the routine may become too long.

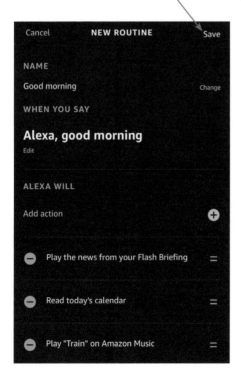

Asking Alexa's Opinion

In addition to asking Alexa to perform specific tasks, such as playing a song or answering a factual question, you can also ask Alexa a range of questions that require an opinion. This may not always result in the expected answer, or any answer at all, but it can be fun asking Alexa a selection of random questions. Some to try include:

- "Alexa, how are you?"

- "Alexa, am I attractive?"

- "Alexa, do you like me?"

- "Alexa, what do you look like?"

- "Alexa, how old are you?"

- "Alexa, what's the meaning of life?"

- "Alexa, what's your favorite tablet?"

- "Alexa, what do you eat?"

- "Alexa, what's your favorite book?" (Alexa can be a bit fickle and if you ask this several times you may get a different answer each time; similarly, when asking Alexa about items such as favorite song, movie, TV show, opera or meal.)

94

What's your favorite book

"Frankenstein" by Mary Shelley is timeless and my personal favorite. I learned a lot from it about what it means to be human.

What's your favorite book?

I thought "The Martian", by Andy Weir, was a thrilling tale. I love the idea of using new technology to solve big problems, like growing potatoes on Mars. I guess you can teach an old spud new tricks!

6 Setting Useful Reminders and Alerts

Alexa can be used to issue reminders and alerts for anything, from taking medication to party invitations. This chapter shows how to set these up.

About Alexa Reminders

Reminders can be set for Alexa, so that they are announced at specific times, either daily or weekly. This is an excellent way to be kept reminded about a range of tasks, from taking regular medication to paying bills. Reminders can be accessed and created in the Alexa app:

1 Open the Alexa app

2 Tap on the **Menu** button

3 Tap on the **Reminders & Alarms** button

4 Tap on the **Reminders** tab

5 Tap on the **Add Reminder** button

6 The template for the reminder contains fields for adding the required content

Don't forget

Reminders can also be added directly via Alexa. However, it can be beneficial to see the content as it is being added, rather than having to speak it all.

7 Tap here and enter the name for the reminder. This will be used by Alexa when the reminder is due

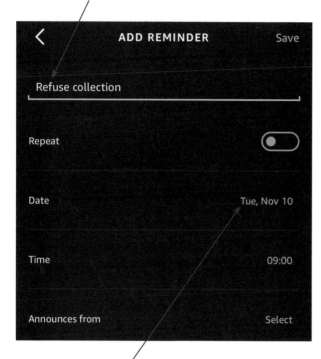

The elements of a reminder, such as the date and time, can be amended once it has been created – see page 104 for details.

Hot tip

8 Tap on the **Date** field and drag on the month, day and year barrels to set the date

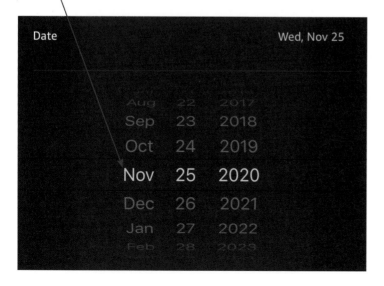

...cont'd

9 Tap on the **Time** field and drag on the hour and minute barrels to set the time for the reminder

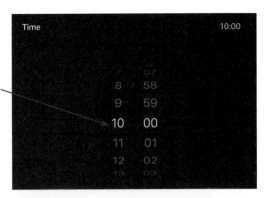

10 To set a recurring reminder, tap on the **Repeat** button so that it is **On**

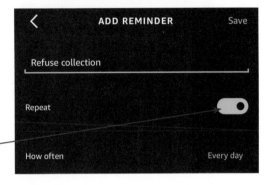

Don't forget

When a button is in the **On** state within the Reminders section, it is light blue.

11 Tap on an item for the recurring reminder. This can be Every day, Weekdays, Weekends or a specific day

...cont'd

12 Tap on the **Announces from** field in Step 7 on page 97, and tap on the device to be used for the reminder – i.e. the one that will announce the reminder

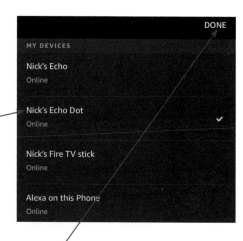

13 Tap on the **Done** button

14 The details of the reminder are listed. Check them for accuracy and tap on an item to edit it

15 Tap on the **Save** button to save the reminder details

16 The reminder is listed on the main **Reminders & Alarms** page

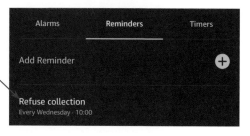

Reminders can only be announced on one device at a time. However, if the reminder is edited, another device can be selected for announcing the reminder.

Useful Regular Reminders

Using Alexa for reminders is a very useful way to make sure that you never miss a range of activities that you do daily, through the week, at the weekends, or weekly. Some of the areas in which you can use Alexa for reminders are:

Regular medication

If you have to take any medication on a regular basis, set a reminder accordingly, for either a daily item:

Only set reminders for taking medication that match the recommended frequency provided by your doctor or pharmacist.

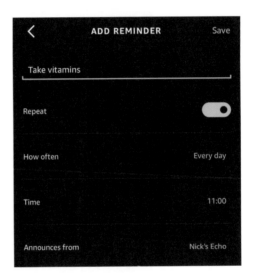

or a weekly one:

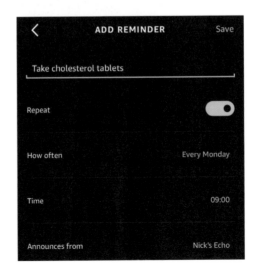

Weekday activities

For something that you have to do every weekday, such as picking up the grandkids from school, set a reminder accordingly, which will be announced Monday to Friday.

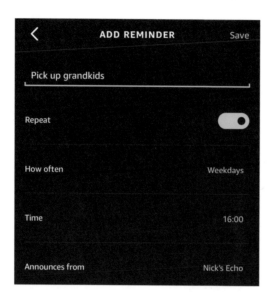

Hot tip

If you are setting a reminder for an event that requires you to travel somewhere to get there, set the reminder for a suitable amount of time before you need to arrive for the event.

Paying weekly bills

If you have any bills that need to be paid on a weekly basis, a reminder can be added for them.

...cont'd

Social engagements

If you have a regular social engagement, such as meeting up with a friend for a sporting activity, this can be added as a reminder at the appropriate time – e.g. at the weekend.

Hot tip

If you may be away from home at the time of an event, set the **Announces from** option to **Alexa on this Phone**, so that the reminder will be announced from your smartphone, rather than an Echo device.

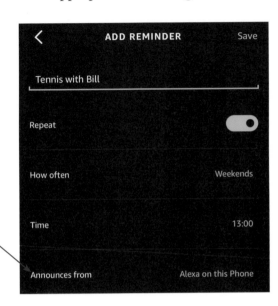

Reminders could also be set for weekly social engagements, such as a weekly book club.

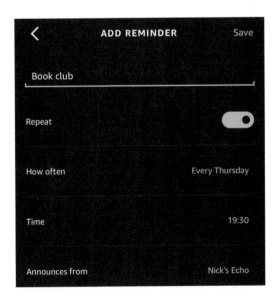

Deleting Reminders

If you do not want to use a reminder anymore it can be deleted altogether. To do this:

1 Tap on the **Reminders** tab in the **Reminders & Alarms** section. Swipe from right to left on a reminder

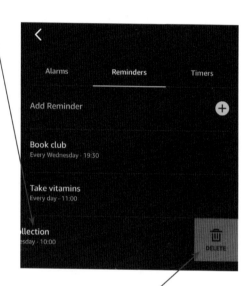

2 Tap on the **Delete** button

3 The reminder is removed from the current list and confirmation is listed at the top of the window

Hot tip

Reminders can also be deleted by Alexa by saying: "Alexa, delete [reminder name]". Alexa will ask for confirmation and then cancel the reminder.

Completing Reminders

If a reminder has a natural end-point, it can be marked as completed and removed from the main Reminders & Alarms section to a Completed section. This works best with one-off reminders. To do this:

1 Tap on the **Reminders** tab in the **Reminders & Alarms** section to view the current reminders

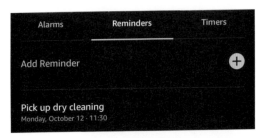

Hot tip

When the action in Step 2 is performed, the reminder is removed to the **Completed** section automatically; you do not have to tap on the green bar or the tick symbol.

2 Swipe from left to right on a reminder

3 Tap on the **View Completed** button at the bottom of the window

VIEW COMPLETED (1)

4 All completed reminders are displayed. Tap here to go back to the main Reminders window

COMPLETED

Pick up dry cleaning
Monday, October 12 · 11:30

Adding Alarms

If you need to be notified about something, another option is to set an alarm that Alexa will play at the selected time. As with reminders, alarms can be customized in terms of time, date, sounds used, and which Echo device the alarm is played on. To do this:

1 Access the **Reminders & Alarms** section of the Alexa app and tap on the **Alarms** tab

An alarm can be added either before or after an important reminder, to reinforce the reminder.

2 Tap on the **Add Alarm** button

3 Options for customizing the alarm are displayed

...cont'd

4 Tap on this button and drag the hour and minute barrels to set the time for the alarm

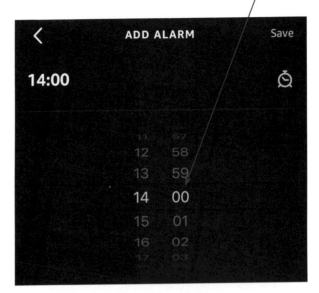

5 Tap on the **Device** button in Step 3 on page 107, and tap on a device on which the alarm will be played. Tap on the **Done** button

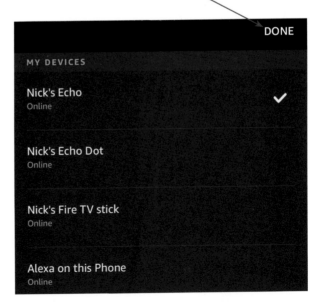

Hot tip

Each alarm can only be applied to one Echo device. However, after one alarm has been created, another one with the same settings can be created and applied to a different Echo device.

6 Tap on the **Repeat** button in Step 3 on page 107, and select the frequency for the alarm

7 Tap on the **Date** button in Step 3 and drag the month, day and year barrels to select a date for when the alarm is played

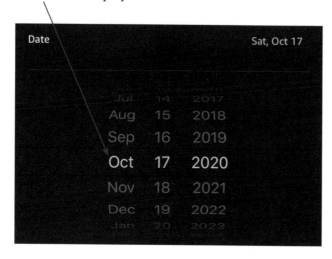

Don't forget

If a repeat option has been selected for the alarm, the date set in Step 7 will be used for the initial occurrence of the alarm.

...cont'd

8 Tap on the **Sound** button in Step 3 on page 107, and tap on a sound to select it for the alarm

9 Review the details of the alarm

Don't forget

An alarm can be deleted in a similar way as for a reminder, by swiping from right to left on the alarm and tapping on the **Delete** button.

10 Tap on the **Save** button to create the alarm

11 The alarm is added in the **Alarms** section of the Reminders & Alarms

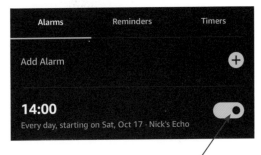

page. Tap on this button to turn an alarm On or Off

Alarm Settings

Settings can be applied for different Echo devices in terms of the alarms that are played on them. This includes customizing the volume and the alarm sound. To do this:

1 Access the **Alarms** tab as shown on page 107, and tap on the **Settings** button at the bottom of the page

`SETTINGS`

2 Tap on a device to which you want to apply specific alarm settings

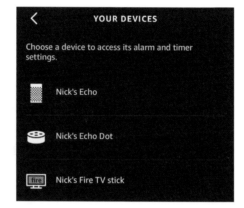

3 Customize the settings for the device as required. This includes setting the volume for the alarm, the alarm sound, and whether it is ascending or not

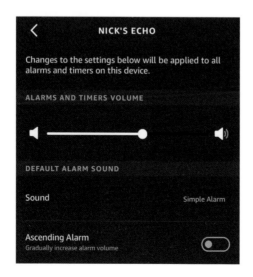

If the **Ascending Alarm** option is turned On in Step 3 on page 107, the alarm will gradually get louder (to a maximum value), until it is stopped.

Setting a Timer

Alexa can be used to set a timer for a specific period of time. This is done with a voice command to Alexa, and the timer is assigned to the Echo device to which the command was delivered. The timer itself can be viewed on the Alexa app. To set a timer:

1 Set a timer with a voice command, such as: "Alexa, set a timer for 10 minutes"

2 Tap on the **Timers** tab in the **Reminders & Alarms** section to view the current timers

A timer can also be paused with the voice command "Alexa, pause timer". The timer can be resumed with the voice command "Alexa, resume timer", or by tapping on the **Play** button in the Alexa app.

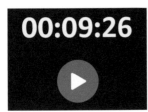

3 Tap on the **Delete** button to remove a timer, or tap on this button to **Pause** it

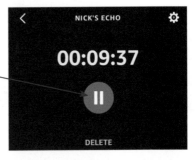

4 Tap on the **Settings** button in the top right-hand corner of the Timers window to access the same settings options as for using alarms

7 Listening to Music

Alexa provides several options for accessing music and playing it through an Echo smart speaker. This chapter looks at these options, including using the Amazon website and the Amazon Music app.

Options for Playing Music

One of the most common uses for the Echo is playing music. The standard Echo and the Echo Plus are excellent for this, since they have high-quality speakers. There are several options for the way you can access music on an Echo:

- Echo devices with Alexa come with access to the Amazon Music library, which is a library of over two million songs that can be streamed over an Echo device.

- Buy specific tracks or albums of music from Amazon and play them from your Amazon Music library. Music that is obtained this way can also be played on a range of devices, including PC, Mac, smartphone, and tablet (iPadOS/iOS and Android).

- Subscribe to Amazon Music Unlimited and stream it to your Echo, over the internet.

- Link to another music subscription service, such as Spotify or Apple Music.

- Listen to radio stations, using the TuneIn radio service or another radio player that is downloaded from the Your Skills section of the Alexa app.

- It is also possible to stream music from an Echo to a connected device – i.e. a Bluetooth speaker.

When playing music, Alexa can perform a range of tasks, such as:

- "Alexa, play [album] by [artist]"

- "Alexa, play next/previous song" (if an album is being played)

- "Alexa, play [song name] by [artist]"

- "Alexa, pause/stop song"

- "Alexa, play songs with Rain in the title"

Amazon Music Unlimited provides access to over 50 million songs.

Audiobooks can also be accessed on Alexa. If you have Kindle books that you have downloaded from Amazon, these can be read out by Alexa. Also, if you have a subscription to Audible, your audiobooks can be read by Alexa. Use the Audible Stories skill to access free content from Audible on Alexa.

Music on the Alexa App

Since an Echo device with Alexa has access to the standard Amazon Music library, this means that music can be played as soon as the Echo and Alexa have been set up. This can be done with the following types of commands:

- "Alexa, play songs by Bruce Springsteen"

- "Alexa, play a summer playlist"

- "Alexa, pick a playlist"

If an item is available with the Amazon Music library, it will start playing on the Echo and the item will also be displayed in the Alexa app. Information can be viewed within the app:

1 Open the Alexa app. If a song is playing, it is displayed above the bottom toolbar

The song details are displayed above the bottom toolbar in the Alexa app, regardless of which option is selected – e.g. Home, Communicate, Play or Devices.

2 Tap on the song name in Step 1 to view more details about it and access the music controls (see page 116)

...cont'd

3 Use these buttons to, from left to right: shuffle the current list of songs; play previous song; pause/play; play next song; and loop the current list of songs

Music played from Amazon Music is streamed over the selected device – i.e. it is played over the internet from the Amazon location on which it is stored: it is not downloaded onto the device on which it is being played.

4 Tap on this button to view the current list of songs being played

5 Tap on this button to access the volume controls and change the volume by dragging on the slider, or by tapping on one of the volume icons at either side of the volume indicator

Accessing music on the Alexa app

Music being played can be viewed in the Alexa app, and items can be selected to play here. To do this:

1 Tap on the **Play** button on the bottom toolbar. The page displays details of music and books that have been played and can be accessed. This includes **Recently Played** items at the top of the page

Play

2 Swipe along the Amazon Music section to view suggested items for playing on an Echo device. Tap on one to play it

Tap on the **Open App** button in Step 1 to open the Amazon Music app for accessing more music, or to download it. See pages 120-125 for details about using the Amazon Music app.

Swipe up the screen in Step 1 to view Kindle books or audiobooks that can be read by Alexa.

117

Music from the Amazon Website

Music can be obtained from Amazon for playing via an Echo device. This is done in two ways: using the Amazon website or the Amazon Music app.

Music can be bought from the Amazon website and then accessed in a variety of ways, including via Alexa. It can also be played on a smartphone or tablet using the Amazon Music app. To obtain music from the Amazon website:

Before you buy any new music from the Amazon website, check that it is not already available with Amazon Music on an Echo device with Alexa.

1 Access the Amazon website and search for an item of music or access it within the Amazon Music **Download Store** section

> Download Store ▾

2 Access the required track or album and tap on the **MP3** option to download a digital version of the item

> Buy MP3 Album £8.99

3 To view items that you have bought, click on the **Account & Lists** button at the right-hand side of the top toolbar, and click on the **Your Music** button

> Hello, Nick
> **Account & Lists** ▾   Returns
> **& Orders**
>
> **Your Account**
>
> Your Account
> Your Orders
> Your Dash Buttons
> Your Lists
> Your Recommendations
> Your Subscribe & Save Items
> Your Pets
> Memberships & Subscriptions
> Your Prime Membership
> Register for a Business Account
>
> Manage Your Content and Devices
> Your Kindle Unlimited
> Your Music Subscriptions
> Your Music

4 The left-hand navigation panel can be used to browse for new music and also access items that you have already purchased. Tap on the item in the main window to play it on the Amazon website

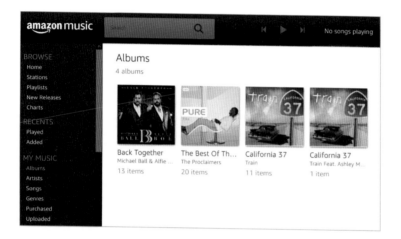

5 A selected item displays the tracks that are available (for an album). Tap on the **Play** button to play the whole album or tap on individual tracks to play them

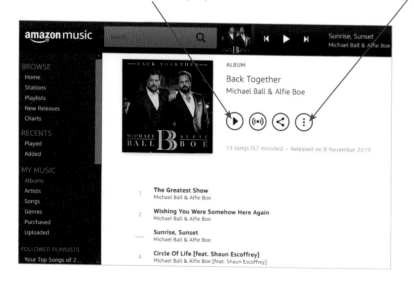

Tap on this button and tap on the **Download** option to download the selected item onto the device on which you are viewing it. This means that it can be played at any time, not just when you are connected to the internet.

Remove from My Music
Download

Music from the Music App

The Amazon Music app is a very flexible way of having access to the vast selection available in the Amazon Music library. The app can be used on a smartphone or a tablet so that you can ensure that Amazon Music is always only a couple of taps away. It can also be used to play music directly to an Echo device with Alexa. To use the Amazon Music app:

1 Access the Amazon Music app from either the Apple App Store or the Google Play Store, depending on the device being used

Hot tip

If you do not already have one, an Amazon account can be created by tapping on the **Create a new Amazon account** button in Step 3.

2 Download the Amazon Music app to your device and tap on it to open it

3 Sign in to the Amazon Music app using your Amazon account details and tap on the **Sign-In** button

4 Tap on the **Home** button on the bottom toolbar

5 The featured music and playlists are displayed. This content is part of the Amazon Music library, which can also be accessed directly on an Echo device with Alexa

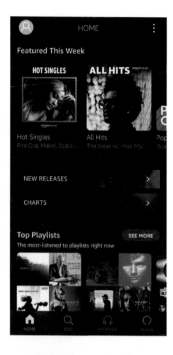

Hot tip

Items within the Amazon Music app can be played on an Echo device, using a voice command such as "Alexa, play 70s pop classics".

121

6 Swipe up the page to view more content, including recommended radio stations and playlists, which are created automatically within the Amazon Music library

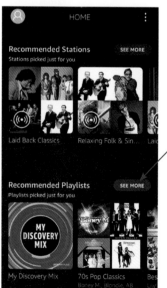

Don't forget

Tap on the **See More** button next to a category to view the full range of options.

...cont'd

7 Tap on the **Find** button on the bottom toolbar to search for specific items

8 Tap in the **Search** box at the top of the window to enter words or phrases for looking for music or artists, or tap on one of the main categories to view the items within them

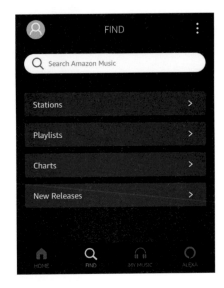

Hot tip

Once music is playing on the Amazon Music app on a smartphone or a tablet, it can then be redirected to play on an Echo device. See page 126 for details about how to do this.

9 Tap on one of the items on the Amazon Music app to play it

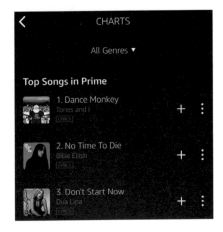

10 Tap on the **My Music** button on the bottom toolbar

11 Items that have been bought through Amazon are listed. Tap on an item to view its details

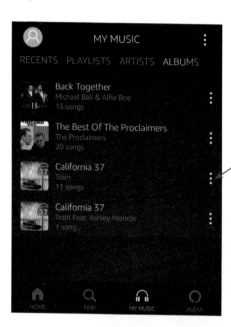

Hot tip

Tap on this button next to an item to access a menu of options related to it. These include: playing other tracks in the music queue; downloading an item onto the device on which you are viewing the Amazon Music app; adding it to a playlist; or sharing it, by sending someone a link to it using email or text message.

123

12 Tap on the **Alexa** button on the bottom toolbar and tap on the **Allow Microphone Access** button to enable using Alexa with the Amazon Music app

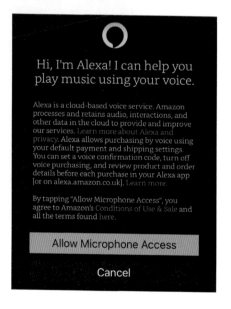

Hi, I'm Alexa! I can help you play music using your voice.

Alexa is a cloud-based voice service. Amazon processes and retains audio, interactions, and other data in the cloud to provide and improve our services. Learn more about Alexa and privacy. **Alexa allows purchasing by voice using your default payment and shipping settings.** You can set a voice confirmation code, turn off voice purchasing, and review product and order details before each purchase in your Alexa app [or on alexa.amazon.co.uk]. Learn more.

By tapping "Allow Microphone Access", you agree to Amazon's Conditions of Use & Sale and all the terms found here.

Allow Microphone Access

Cancel

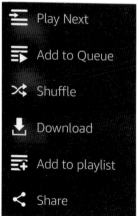

Play Next

Add to Queue

Shuffle

Download

Add to playlist

Share

Music on the Music App

Once music has been accessed in the Amazon Music app it can be played on the device on which the app is downloaded, and also on an Echo device. To do this:

Playing music on the Music app

1 Access the required item within the Amazon Music app, as shown on page 117

Don't forget

New playlists are created in the Amazon Music library on a regular basis.

2 Tap on the item in Step 1 to view the tracks within it – e.g. for an album or a playlist

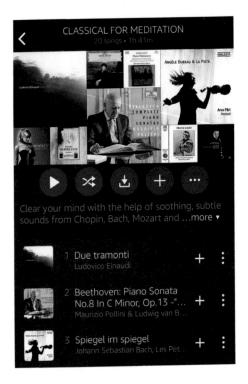

3 Tap on this button to play the whole album or playlist, in the order shown

4 Tap on these buttons in Step 2 on the previous page to, from left to right: play the current track, album or playlist; shuffle the selected items; download the track, album or playlist to your device; add the track, album or playlist to your My Music section; and access the **More** options (see next step)

5 The options on the **More** button include: playing an item; following it (i.e. adding it to your My Music section); sharing it; and playing any related radio stations

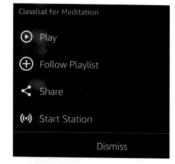

6 When an track is being played, the music interface is displayed. Use the music controls to play the previous track, play or pause the current track, or play the next track

7 Use the buttons at the bottom of the screen to, from left to right: repeat an item; view the full track list; ask Alexa to play an item; select another location for playing the current track; or shuffle the track list

125

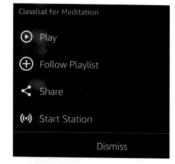

Don't forget

See page 126 for details about selecting another location for playing an item.

From Music App to Echo

Music on the Amazon Music app does not have to be restricted to the device on which the app has been downloaded. It is possible to stream music that is playing on the Music app to an Echo device with Alexa. To do this:

Don't forget

It is also possible to connect to an Echo device from the homepage of the Amazon Music app. To do this, tap on the **Menu** button, tap on the **Connect to a Device** button, and tap on the required device as in Step 2.

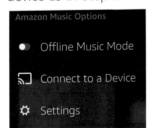

1 Access a track on the Music app so that it is playing on the device on which the app has been downloaded. Tap on this button at the bottom of the window in Step 7 on page 125

2 Select the device on which you want the music to be played

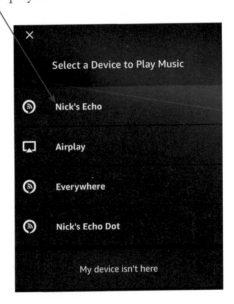

3 Open the Alexa app and tap on the **Play** button on the bottom toolbar to see the currently-playing item

Music App Settings

There are various settings within the Amazon Music app that can be used to determine how it works. To access these:

1 Open the Amazon Music app, tap on the **Menu** button on the homepage, and tap on the **Settings** button

2 Swipe up the page to view the available settings

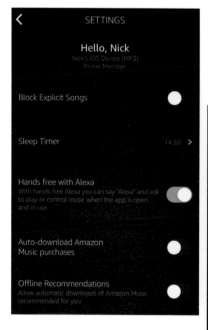

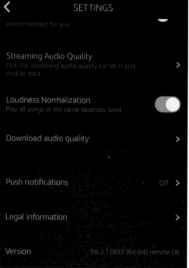

The Push notifications options can be turned **On** in Step 2. However, this could result in a lot of notifications from the Amazon Music app.

...cont'd

3 Turn **On** the **Block Explicit Songs** button in Step 2 (on page 127), and tap on the **Block** button to block any songs that have explicit words in the lyrics

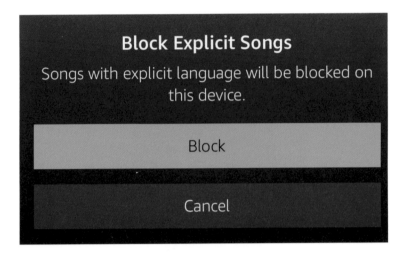

Don't forget

If the Sleep Timer option has been turned **On** at night time, remember to turn it **Off** again during the day.

4 Tap on the **Sleep Timer** button in Step 2, then tap **On** the **Sleep Timer** option and select a duration for when music stops playing

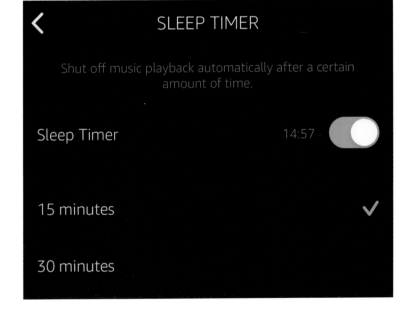

5 Tap on the **Streaming Audio Quality** button in Step 2 (on page 127), and drag the **Stream only on Wi-Fi** button **On** to ensure that music is only streamed from Amazon Music when your device is connected to Wi-Fi

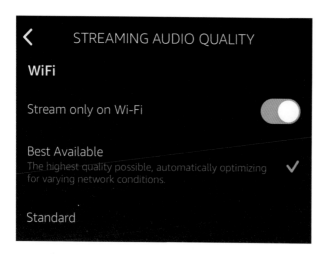

6 Tap on the **Download Audio Quality** button in Step 2, and drag the **Download only on Wi-Fi** button **On** to ensure that music can only be downloaded from Amazon Music when your device is connected to Wi-Fi

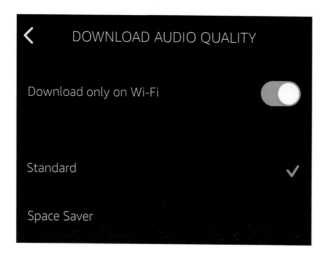

If the **Streaming Audio Quality** or **Download Audio Quality** options are not turned **On**, music could be streamed or downloaded using 3G, 4G or 5G on your device, which could result in data charges, depending on your data plan.

Music on the Radio

For radio lovers, Alexa uses the TuneIn radio service to provide a huge range of local, national and international radio stations, covering music, talk radio, sports and news. This is a built-in skill with Alexa, so nothing has to be done to use it, other than asking Alexa to play a specific radio station. In addition, other radio players can also be used. To listen to music on the radio:

Don't forget

The currently-playing station can be paused or played by tapping on the **Pause/Play** icon at the bottom of the screen. The volume can also be amended by tapping on the speaker icon.

1 Say: "Alexa, play radio Country 104". Open the Alexa app. At the top of the homepage is the currently-playing radio station from TuneIn

2 Tap at the bottom of the screen to view more details about the currently-playing item and access the music controls

Searching for radio players

In addition to TuneIn, other radio players can be used with Alexa on an Echo device. To do this:

1 Open the Alexa app and access the **Skills & Games** section as shown on page 54. Tap on the Search icon at the top of the page and enter a search word or phrase into the Search box. The relevant radio player skills are displayed

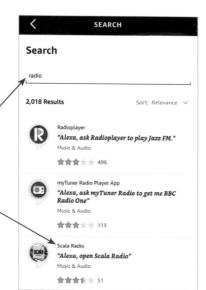

The Search icon is located in the top right-hand corner on the **Skills & Games** homepage.

SKILLS & GAMES   Q

131

2 Tap on one of the radio player skills to review its details, including Alexa voice commands that can be used with it. Tap on the **Enable To Use** button to activate the radio player so that it can be used with Alexa on an Echo device

More Music Services

Another way of playing music on an Echo device with Alexa is by connecting to an existing streaming service. This involves playing music over the internet with a service such as Apple Music or Spotify. To do this:

Beware

The Apple Music and Deezer options can be activated by enabling the relevant skill, once the buttons in Step 2 have been tapped. However, although the skill can be enabled, the service will only be available if you have a subscription with the selected service.

1 Open the Alexa app and tap on the **Play** button on the bottom toolbar

2 Swipe to the bottom of the page to view the available music services

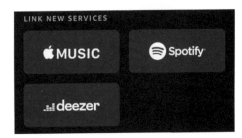

3 Tap on a music service to link to it. You need to have an existing account with the selected music service in order to use it with Alexa on an Echo device. Enter your login details for the account, or download the app for the service and create a new account through the app

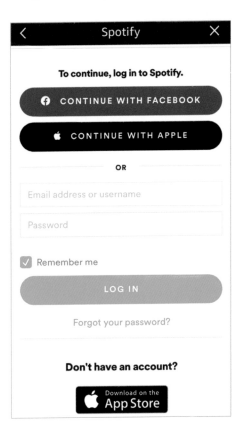

Selecting a default music service

If you have linked to more than one music streaming service, which is perfectly possible, a default one has to be specified. This will be the music library that Alexa will look in first when you make a request for playing an item of music. To specify a default music service:

1 Access the **Play** section of the Alexa app as in Step 1 on the previous page. Swipe to the bottom of the page and tap on the **Manage Your Services** button

The default music service is the one that Alexa will use when you ask music to be played. If you want to use a specific service (if you are linked to more than one), say: "Alexa, play [music name] from [music service name, e.g. Apple Music]".

2 The current music services are listed

3 Tap on the **Default Services** option

New services can also be linked to by tapping on the **Link New Service** button in Step 2.

4 Tap on a service to make it the default one, if there is more than one available. The default one is denoted by a check mark symbol next to it

133

Using Bluetooth Speakers

An Echo device can be linked to an external Bluetooth speaker, so this can be used as an output device for Alexa commands and responses. This has to be with a separate Bluetooth device that has to be "paired" with the Echo so that the two devices can communicate with each other. This is done through the Alexa app:

The Bluetooth device has to be in pairing mode before it can be paired with the Echo device – consult the user instructions for details about accessing this mode. In some cases, this can be as simple as turning the device **On**.

1 Open the Alexa app and tap on the **Devices** button on the bottom toolbar

2 Tap on the **Echo & Alexa** button at the top of the Devices page

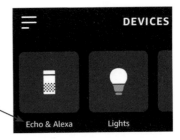

3 Tap on the required Echo device (each device has to be paired separately with a Bluetooth speaker)

Paired devices are listed under the **Wireless** heading in the Echo device's settings, which are accessed by tapping on the required device in Step 3. Tap on the **Bluetooth Devices** button to see details of paired devices.

4 Tap on the **Pair Alexa Gadget** button

Pair Alexa Gadget

5 Tap on the device to be paired. Once this is done, every time the device is turned **On**, the output from the Echo will be played on it, instead of on the Echo device

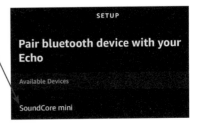

8 Communicating

This chapter details Alexa's communication skills, for making calls and sending messages.

Adding Contacts to Alexa

Alexa can be used to perform a range of communication tasks, such as making a call to a smartphone or sending a text message to a tablet. However, in order for Alexa to be able to do this, there have to be contacts available with which to communicate. This can either be done by giving Alexa access to existing contacts on a smartphone or tablet, or by creating new contacts in the Alexa app.

Using existing contacts

The good news when using Alexa for communication is that you do not have to manually add all of your existing contacts from your smartphone or tablet. Instead, you give Alexa permission to access these contacts. To do this:

Hot tip

The **Amazon Alexa** button appears in the settings of a smartphone or tablet once the Alexa app has been downloaded on the device.

1. On your smartphone or tablet, tap on the **Settings** button

Settings

2. Tap on the **Amazon Alexa** button

Amazon Alexa

3. Drag the **Contacts** button **On** to allow Alexa to have access to the contacts on your smartphone or tablet

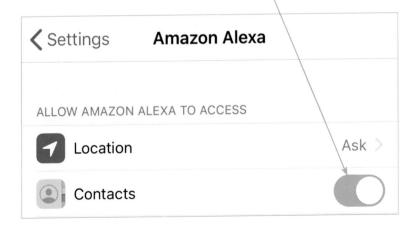

‹ Settings   **Amazon Alexa**

ALLOW AMAZON ALEXA TO ACCESS

◤ Location   Ask ›

◉ Contacts   ⬤

...cont'd

Creating new contacts

Contacts can also be added directly in the Alexa app.

1 Open the Alexa app and tap on the **Menu** button

2 Tap on the **Contacts** button **Contacts**

3 The current contacts are displayed. Tap on this button to add a new one

4 Tap on the **Add Contact** button

When adding contacts, add a mobile number so that Alexa can use it for communicating with that person. The **Mobile** field is further down the page in Step 5.

5 Enter the details for the new contact and tap on the **Save** button

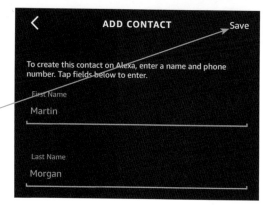

Communication Settings

Before making calls or sending messages, there are some settings within the Alexa app that can be applied to manage certain aspects of your communication with Alexa.

1 Open the Alexa app and tap on the **Communicate** button on the bottom toolbar

2 Tap on this icon in the top right-hand corner of the **Communication** page

The page in Step 3 can also be accessed by tapping on the **Menu** button at the top of any window in the Alexa app, and then tapping on the **Contacts** button.

3 Tap on the **My Communications Settings** option under the Search box

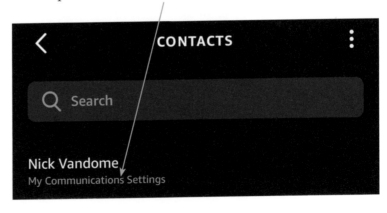

4 The communication settings are displayed

5 Drag the **Show Caller ID** button **On** to enable your own caller ID to be displayed on someone's phone when you make a call to them

The Caller ID name that is displayed is the name that the recipient has assigned to you on their phone; it is not the name that you have assigned in the Alexa app.

6 Drag the **Allow Drop In** button **On** to enable two Echo devices, or an Echo device and the Alexa app, to communicate with each other – see pages 142-143 for details

Calling from Alexa

Alexa can be used to make voice calls to someone's smartphone, either through an Echo device with Alexa or through the Alexa app.

Calling using Alexa on an Echo device

To make a call to someone's smartphone directly from an Echo device with Alexa:

Don't forget

Calls made via Alexa on an Echo device are done over Wi-Fi.

1 Say: "Alexa, call Nick". Alexa will repeat the recipient's name to ensure that you have the correct person. The call is made to the recipient's smartphone, using the contact details added on pages 138-139

2 The recipient taps on the **Accept** button to take the call. Whatever is spoken to the Echo will be heard on the recipient's smartphone

Hot tip

Calls can be made to a named person, but if they have more than one contact number then the specific device has to be used – e.g. "Alexa, call Nick's mobile". Calls can also be made to a specific number – e.g. "Alexa, call 07777 123456".

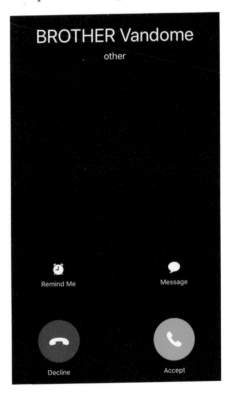

Calling from the Alexa app

To make a call to someone from the Alexa app:

1 Open the Alexa app and tap on the **Communicate** button on the bottom toolbar

2 Tap on the **Call** button

3 Tap on a contact in the list of contacts in the Alexa app

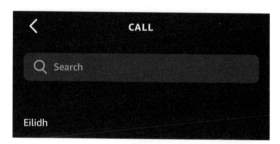

Hot tip

Making calls from a smartphone using the Alexa app is a good option if your normal call provider is not available for any reason.

4 If there is more than one number for the contact, tap on the one to use

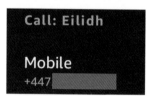

5 Tap on the **Call** button to call the number

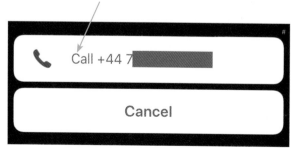

Dropping In

Within the home, the Echo is an excellent option for creating an internal intercom system. It is possible to communicate between Echo devices in different rooms in the home, and also from the Alexa app to an Echo device. This is known as Drop In. To use this:

Hot tip

If you use the Alexa app, you can drop in to an Echo device in your home, from any location.

1 Open the Alexa app and tap on the **Communicate** button

2 Tap on the **Drop In** button

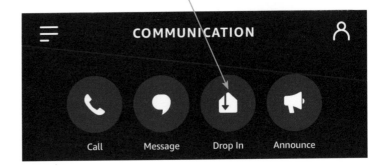

3 Tap on the device you want to drop in on

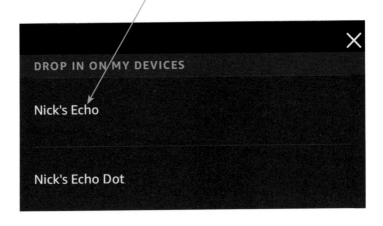

4 Once the connection is made, you can communicate with the Echo in the same way as for making a phone call. Tap on this button to alter the volume

Nick's Echo

To finish a Drop In conversation from the Alexa app, tap on the red button in Step 4. To finish it from one Echo device to another, say: "Alexa, hang up".

143

If you are using Drop In between two Echo devices, make sure that the volume is at a sufficient level on each one, so that both people can hear each other adequately.

5 Tap on this button to mute a Drop In call, so that it cannot be heard on the Echo device

6 Drop In can also be used between Echo devices by saying: **"Alexa, drop in on [Echo name]"**, which is a great way to communicate between Echo devices throughout the home

Messaging with Alexa

It is possible to send text messages using an Echo device or the Alexa app. However, to do this, the recipient must also have an Echo device or the Alexa app. Messages can be sent from the Alexa app or an Echo device:

Messages from the Alexa app
To send a text message from the Alexa app:

1 Open the Alexa app, then tap on the **Communicate** button

2 Tap on the **Message** button

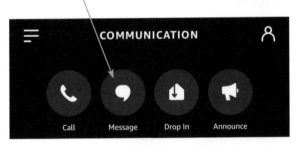

Beware

Even if people are in your full list of contacts on the Alexa app, they will only appear on the list in Step 3 if they have an Echo device or the Alexa app, and can be contacted via messaging.

3 A list of contacts is displayed. This is people in your Contacts list who have an Echo device or Alexa app. Tap on a name to send that person a message

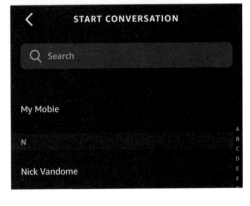

4 Tap in the text box and type the message

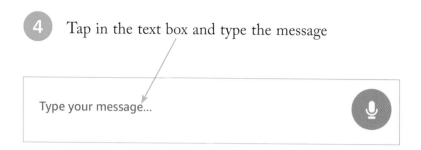

Type your message...

5 Tap on this button to send the message

Hi, when shall we meet?

6 The message appears in the recipient's Alexa app and it can also be played from an Echo device by saying: "Alexa, play message"

11:16 AM

Hi, when shall we meet?

7 Tap on the microphone icon in Step 4 to record a voice message that can be viewed in the Alexa app and also accessed from an Echo device by saying: "Alexa, play message"

Type your message...

Hot tip

If a voice message is sent via an Echo device, it shows up on the conversation page of the Alexa app with a **Play** button icon. Tap on the icon to hear the voice message.

▶ Play Message
This is sent by an echo

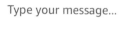

...cont'd

Messages from Alexa on an Echo device

To send a text message to someone hands-free, using a voice command to Alexa on an Echo device:

1 Say: "Alexa, send a message to Nick". Alexa on the Echo device will ask what message you want to send. Tell Alexa the required message (you do not have to precede this with "Alexa"), and say: "send message"

2 If a message has been delivered and is waiting to be accessed, the ring at the top of the standard Echo and the Echo Dot pulses yellow

Don't forget

When a message is first delivered, the Echo will emit a sound to alert you to the new message.

Don't forget

The ring on the Echo device continues to pulse yellow until the message is accessed.

3 The message can be played on the recipient's Echo device by saying: "Alexa, play message"

9 Online Shopping

This chapter details shopping with Alexa.

About Voice Shopping

Beware

You have to be a member of Amazon Prime to use voice shopping with Alexa.

Don't forget

If you are using an Echo device with a screen (e.g. the Echo Show or the Echo Spot), Alexa can display shopping items on the screen, by asking: "Alexa, show me washing powder".

Hot tip

Alexa works most effectively for voice shopping on the Amazon website. However, skills can be added for other voice-shopping options, but they only work with retailers who are signed up for voice shopping via Alexa.

Amazon is one of the major online retailers on the web. Using your Echo and Alexa, you can make use of this valuable resource and order eligible items using voice purchasing by asking Alexa. This is done with voice purchasing with Alexa, and 1-Click purchasing through your Amazon account. To view information about voice purchasing on the Alexa app:

1 Open the Alexa app and tap on the **Menu** button

2 Tap on the **Things to Try** button

Things to Try

3 Tap on the **Shopping** button

Shopping

4 Details about using voice shopping are displayed. Tap on the **Enable Voice Shopping** button to set up voice shopping with Alexa – see next page

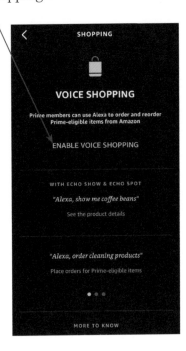

Setting Up Voice Shopping

There a few steps to take to set up voice shopping. Once this has been done, shopping on Amazon can be done with voice commands to Alexa. To set up voice shopping:

1 Tap on the **Enable Voice Shopping** button on the previous page, or select **Menu > Settings > Account Settings > Voice Purchasing**. Both methods access the **Voice Purchasing** page

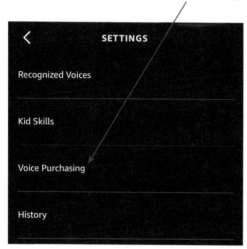

2 Tap the **Purchase by voice** button **On**

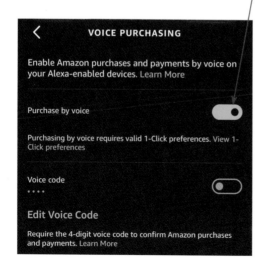

Don't forget

To prevent any voice purchasing from Alexa on an Echo device, tap on the **Purchase by voice** button in Step 2 so that it is **Off**.

...cont'd

Hot tip

1-Click shopping is initially set up on the Amazon website once you have logged in with your Amazon account details. Once 1-Click shopping has been set up, you do not need to enter your payment details every time you buy something from Amazon.

Don't forget

Tap on the **Back** button in Step 4 to go back to the main Voice Purchasing page.

3 Tap on the **View 1-Click preferences** link in Step 2 on page 149

Purchasing by voice requires valid 1-Click preferences. View 1-Click preferences

4 The current details for 1-Click shopping are displayed. Tap on the **Edit Payment Method** button to change the card details that are currently being used for 1-Click payments, if required

<

Payment Settings

All Kindle transactions are completed with 1-Click. Changes made to your default 1-Click method will apply to future Amazon.co.uk 1-Click transactions, but will not change your current active subscriptions.

Your Default 1-Click Payment Method
Visa/Delta/Electron ending in *

Edit Payment Method ⤢

5 Tap on the **Voice code** button

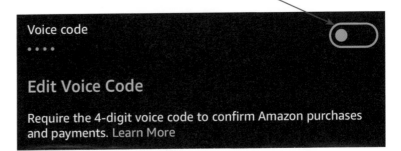

Voice code
• • • •

Edit Voice Code

Require the 4-digit voice code to confirm Amazon purchases and payments. Learn More

6 Enter a four-digit code and tap on the **Save** button

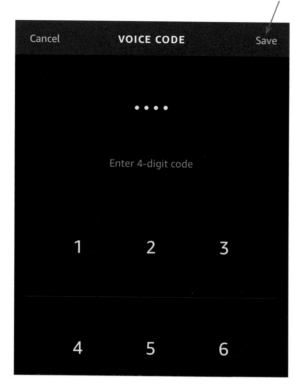

If a voice code is added, Alexa will ask for it when you make a voice purchase.

7 Once a voice code has been added, the **Recognize Speakers** option is available on the Voice Purchasing page. Tap on this to turn it **On**, if you want voice purchasing to override the voice code if it recognizes your voice – i.e. the voice code will not be required

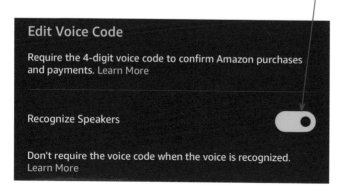

Using Voice Shopping

Once Alexa has been set up for voice shopping, you can start making purchases on Amazon, using voice commands.

It is possible to ask Alexa to buy a generic item – e.g. "Alexa, buy coffee beans". In this instance, the information will be displayed on the Amazon website in your basket. Tap on the **Choose Item** button for Amazon to suggest an item based on the original voice command.

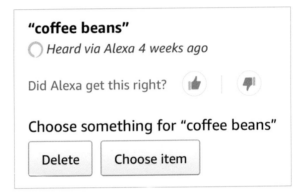

Beware

If a voice code is not added, as on pages 150-151, anyone in your home could make voice purchases on Amazon using Alexa, without your knowledge.

If you use a voice command for a specific item, Alexa will repeat the details and place the item in your Amazon basket, where you can review it and buy it if required. The item can also be bought by using the voice command "Alexa, buy now", after Alexa has reviewed the request.

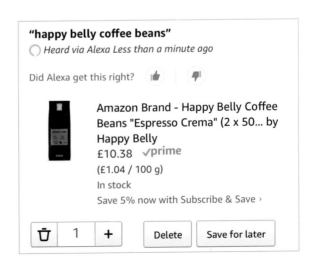

10 Alexa and the Smart Home

Smart home devices are becoming increasingly popular. These are devices that can be controlled with apps, and also with smart speakers that have digital voice assistants like Alexa. This chapter shows how to do it.

About the Alexa Smart Home

The idea of a smart home – i.e. one in which functions within the home can be controlled by computer devices – is no longer in the realms of science fiction: it is very much a reality and within reach of everyone.

The Echo and Alexa can be put at the heart of a smart home, in terms of being able to control devices through voice commands – e.g. turning on the lights or adjusting the thermostat. Some of the types of devices that can be controlled with Alexa include:

- **Lighting**. Smart lighting systems can be installed without the need for an electrician or electrical expertise, so that lights can be turned on and off with Alexa. They can also be dimmed and, with colored smart lighting sets, different color themes can be applied.

- **Heating**. Smart thermostats can be used to control central heating by changing the temperature or turning it on or off. The temperature can be controlled using voice commands to Alexa.

Hot tip

Installing smart lighting may seem like a daunting prospect, but it can be surprisingly straightforward, and is very rewarding once it is up and running. See pages 160-161 for details.

Don't forget

Smart lighting and heating have to be set up with their own apps before they can be used with Alexa.

- **Locks and security systems**. Some smart house security devices can be controlled by Alexa to keep your property secure. These include individual security cameras, and also comprehensive security systems for the whole home.

- **Sockets and plugs**. These can be controlled so that devices can be turned on and off around the home. For instance, a kettle can be connected using a smart plug so that it can be controlled hands-free, with a voice command via the smart plug.

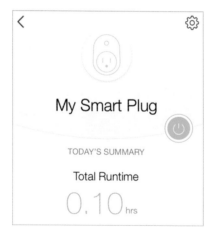

My Smart Plug

TODAY'S SUMMARY

Total Runtime

0.10 hrs

- **Curtains/drapes**. Instead of having to open and close curtains/drapes manually, a smart system can be used to automatically open or close them when the appropriate command is made to Alexa.

- **A range of accessories** – including air conditioners, humidifiers, fans and speakers.

Smart devices require access to some form of wireless communication (usually Wi-Fi), and they can be controlled with an appropriate app on a smartphone or tablet.

Don't forget

Devices that are controlled by a smart plug, such as a kettle, have to be left on in order for them to be turned on and off via the smart plug.

155

Beware

Smart home devices have to go through their own setup process before they can be controlled through Alexa.

Adding Smart Home Skills

Smart home gadgets can be controlled with their own companion app, and relevant skills for a gadget can also be added to Alexa to make it possible for Alexa to communicate with the gadget. This is done once the smart home gadget has been installed and set up with its own app. Most smart home gadgets have their own Alexa skill. To add smart home skills:

Smart home devices have their own skills for Alexa. However, other skills can also be used with a range of smart home devices: you do not need a specific skill from the manufacturer of the smart home device.

1 Open the Alexa app and access **Menu > Skills & Games**

Skills & Games

2 Tap on the Search icon and search for smart home skills. Swipe up the page to view the full list of available skills

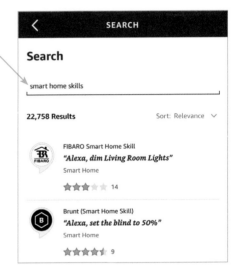

3 It is also possible to search for a skills for a specific smart home product – e.g. the Philips Hue smart lighting system

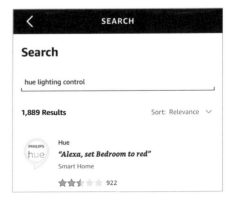

4 Tap on the required skill and tap on the **Enable To Use** button to add it to Alexa. This will act as a companion to the related smart home gadget. Without it, Alexa will not be able to communicate with the smart gadget

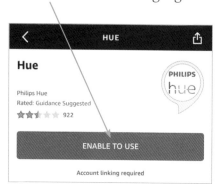

5 For some smart home devices, you will have to link to its manufacturer's website, which is done through the Alexa app. Tap on the **Enable To Use** button in Step 4, and link to the account with an email address and a password, or use your login details for another account, such as a Google account. This provides greater functionality with the smart home device

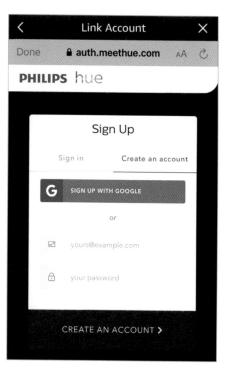

Once you have linked a skill to the online account, Alexa will ask for permission to use the device. Tap on the **Yes** button to give this permission.

About Smart Lighting

Smart lighting is one of the most accessible and striking options for adding smart devices to the home: it can be set up in a matter of minutes, does not need an electrician (or any electrical knowledge), and creates a dramatic impact once it is up and running. Smart lighting also works impressively with Alexa.

Elements of smart lighting

The good news about a smart lighting system is that all of the components can be linked to existing elements of your home, and there is no need to alter any current equipment. Smart lighting works through a controller (bridge) that is connected to your Wi-Fi router, and the smart light bulbs are then controlled by Wi-Fi through the bridge. The elements required for a smart lighting system include:

Smart light bulbs contain a considerable amount of technology and are more expensive than standard light bulbs. Single white bulbs are upward of £10/$10.

- **Smart light bulbs.** These are light bulbs that can communicate using Wi-Fi via the smart lighting bridge. They can be either white, or white and colored, in which case they can change color and also create artistic scenes if more than one bulb is used in a particular room. Smart light bulbs are installed in exactly the same way as for regular bulbs, either with a bayonet fitting or a screw fitting into the light socket.

- **Bridge**. This is the controller that is connected to your Wi-Fi router. Once it has been set up, this is where commands will be sent (either through a related app or a voice-controlled device, such as Alexa) and then distributed to the smart lighting system.

The bridge is connected to the Wi-Fi router with an Ethernet cable, which is usually supplied with the bridge.

- **Remote control**. In addition to controlling the smart lighting through an app or Alexa, it can also be controlled with a remote control. This can be used to turn the lights on or off and dim them as required. If you have a group of smart lights in one room, the remote control can

usually only be used with the whole group, rather than controlling individual lights separately.

Setting Up Smart Lighting

Smart lighting has a number of elements to it, and there are a few steps that have to be done before it can be used and controlled via Alexa. (The examples here are for the popular Philips Hue smart lighting system, but the process is similar for most major smart lighting options.)

Hot tip

If you buy a smart lighting starter kit, this should include white or colored smart light bulbs and the bridge for connecting the system. Otherwise, the bridge can be bought separately. There is a wide range of smart lighting products on the Amazon website.

1 Insert the smart light bulbs and turn the lights On at the wall light switch and the lamp switch (if applicable)

2 Plug in the bridge and connect it to your Wi-Fi router using the supplied Ethernet cable

3 Download the related app, from either the Apple App Store or the Google Play Store, to your smartphone or tablet

Philips Hue
Philips Lighting BV

GET

2.6 ★★★☆☆
268 Ratings

4 Open the app. It should locate the bridge automatically. Tap on the **Set up** button

1 new Hue bridge found

Set up

5 Press the main button on the bridge to link it to the app. Once this is linked, any commands made regarding the smart lighting will go through the bridge

Smart lighting can be controlled effectively using its own companion app. However, Alexa is the best option if you want to control your smart lighting with voice commands.

6 Tap on the **+** button to set up lights in specific rooms, so they can communicate with the bridge

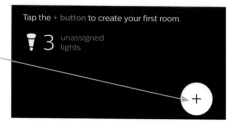

7 Enter a name for the room (or use the default name already provided) and tap on the checkbox for the lights that you want to include in that room. Tap on the **Save** button to complete the room setup

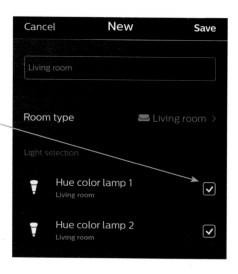

161

Setting Up a Room

Once a smart lighting system has been set up and light bulbs have been added, rooms can be set up with the relevant light bulbs assigned to them. Once this has been done, Alexa can be given commands to control the lighting in a specific room. To do this:

Don't forget

Once smart light bulbs have been installed and turned on, the light switch can be left on: all of the functionality of the bulb can be controlled through the light's app.

1 Open the smart lighting app

2 Tap on the **Home** button on the bottom toolbar

3 Tap on the **Create room** button

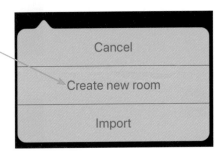

No rooms created

Create rooms and assign lights

Create room

4 Tap on the **Create new room** option

Cancel

Create new room

Import

5 The room is given a default name. To change this, tap on the **Room type** option

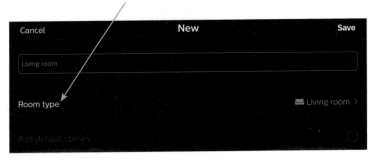

Cancel   New   Save

Living room

Room type   Living room ›

Add default scenes

6 Tap on a room type and tap on the **Back** button

7 Once the room type has been selected, light bulbs can be assigned to the room. Tap in the boxes to select the required light bulbs. Tap on the **Save** button to create the room, with the selected bulbs

Beware

If you move the location of a smart light bulb (e.g. move it from the main light fitting in a room to a side lamp), the name and the functionality will not change. For instance, if the app thinks it is accessing Light 1, this will be unaffected regardless of which fitting the light is placed in, or even which room, if it has been moved to another room.

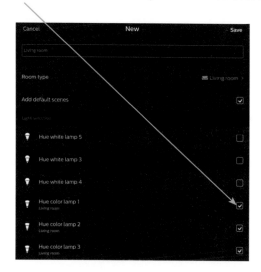

8 The new room is shown on the **Home** page

Using Lights

Individual light bulbs can be used with Alexa in terms of controlling them with voice commands. They can also be controlled using their companion app. To do this:

When smart lights are turned on, they remember the state they were in when they were turned off – i.e. if they were set to be purple, this is the color they will be when they are turned on again.

1   Open the smart lighting app and tap on the **Home** button on the bottom toolbar

2   Drag this button On to turn on all of the smart lights. For Alexa, this can be done with the voice command "Alexa, turn on all lights"

3   Tap on a room name to view details of the lights in the room

...cont'd

4 Tap on this button to view the individual lights in a room

5 Drag the buttons On or Off for individual lights, as required

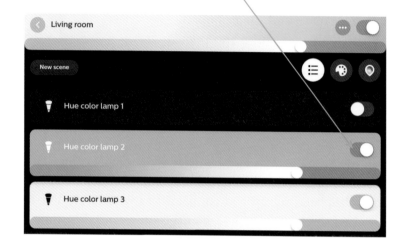

The current color for a light bulb is shown in the window in Step 5.

6 Tap on this button to access available lighting scenes for the room

7 Tap on one of the scene options to apply that for all of the lights in the room

Scenes can only be created with color smart light bulbs.

About Smart Heating

Smart heating systems enable you to control your central heating with a wireless thermostat that can be managed through a related app, or with Alexa. Smart heating can also be controlled remotely, so that you always have the ability to monitor and manage your central heating.

Smart heating works with central heating systems, and the examples here use the widely-used and popular Nest smart heating system.

Hot tip

In some locations, the Nest system can be bought either with or without installation included in the price. If installation is included, a local supplier will contact you about scheduling the installation. For more details, look at the Nest website at nest.com

A smart thermostat should be fitted by a qualified installer (several devices have their own recommended installers), and once it has been set up and connected to your home Wi-Fi, it can be used to control and manage your central heating in a number of different ways:

- Turn your heating on or off (either through an app or by using Alexa).

- Set your smart thermostat to a specific temperature.

- Program your smart thermostat to come on or go off at specific times. This can be as many times as you like during the day.

- Turn your heating on or off remotely (using the app).

- Use an economy setting so that you can keep your heating on without wasting unnecessary energy.

- Apply a frost setting when you are away from home, if you are worried about freezing pipes.

Some smart thermostats can also have settings applied to determine whether you are home or not, and set the temperature accordingly. This helps to save energy, which is one of the benefits of a smart thermostat.

Elements of Smart Heating

Smart heating enables you to control the heating in your home through an app or Alexa. This can be done while you are at home, and also remotely. The elements of a smart heating system include:

1 A heat link thermostat that connects to the central heating boiler. The heating system is then left on at the boiler: all of the controls are done through the heat link thermostat, using an app, a system controller (learning thermostat), or Alexa

The heat link and smart thermostat should be fitted by an approved central heating engineer or gas fitter.

2 A learning thermostat (smart thermostat) that communicates with the heat link connected to the central heating system. The learning thermostat is able to monitor room temperatures and adjust them accordingly

Smart Heating App

A companion app is required to set up and manage a smart heating system (in this case the Nest app, which can be downloaded to a smartphone or a tablet from the Apple App Store or the Google Play Store). To use the app:

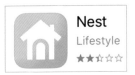

Don't forget

Similar options to those accessible through the app can also be used on the learning thermostat for controlling heating.

1 Open the app and tap on the **Heating** button to access the basic heating controls

2 Tap on the **Heat** button or the **Off** button

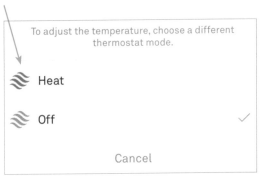

3 Tap on the **Schedule** button on the bottom toolbar to create a schedule for the heating system

SCHEDULE

Hot tip

The app for a smart heating system can be used to turn the heating on or off, even when you are away from home. Also, if you know you are going to be away, you can create an appropriate schedule – i.e. if you know it is going to be particularly cold weather, you can schedule the heating to come on for an hour or two a day, even if you are not there.

4 Tap on the **History** button on the bottom toolbar to view a chart of your energy usage

HISTORY

5 Tap on the **Eco** button on the bottom toolbar to access economy mode

ECO

Don't forget

Once the smart heating app has been downloaded and set up, the relevant skill can be added to Alexa to enable voice commands to be used with the smart heating system.

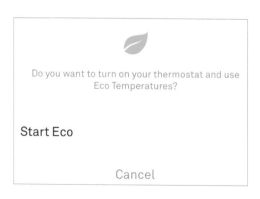

Smart Security

Smart home technology is an excellent way to add a range of security features to your home:

- Full security systems.

- Individual security cameras, for both external and internal use.

- Smart locks.

Full security systems

A full smart security system consists of a number of external cameras (usually three or more) that provide live video feeds of the exterior of your home. This can be viewed – via Wi-Fi – on a desktop computer, a laptop, a tablet, or a smartphone. The cameras should have night-vision capabilities and be weatherproof. Some systems can also record video to a hard drive, but these are more expensive. Alexa can be used with compatible systems to instruct that a specific scene is displayed on the Echo Show (with video screen). External systems with a single camera or a night light are also available.

Beware

A full security system consists of several elements, and it is best to have one installed by a professional, who can also recommend the best options for using it with Alexa.

Individual cameras

For security within the home, individual smart cameras can be used. This is most effective with Alexa and the Echo Show, so that the scene can be viewed on its video screen.

Smart locks

Smart locks can be used with a range of options for unlocking and locking (including using Alexa, which usually has to be done with a hub that connects wirelessly to the lock, in a similar way as to controlling smart lights). The options include: key card; key tag; manual code; smartphone or tablet app; or Alexa. Do not rely solely on smart locks for a way to get into your home. Make sure that you have a manual alternative, in case any of the technology for the lock stops working. Alexa can be used within the home to give you peace of mind by locking all locks before you go to bed.

Beware

Never tell anyone the manual code for a smart lock. If you do have to write it down, keep it somewhere secure, ideally in a home safe.

Smart Plugs

Smart plugs are a small but effective way of controlling electrical devices around the home. They are easy to set up, which can usually be done without the need of a separate hub or bridge connected to your Wi-Fi router. Some options for smart plugs include:

- Turning devices on or off.

- Creating timed schedules to turn devices on or off automatically.

- Checking the status of electronic devices, via the smart plug.

- Using remote access with a companion app.

Once smart plugs have been installed, they can be paired to an Echo, by adding the relevant skill in the Alexa app. Once smart plugs have been installed, they can be linked to Alexa so that they can be activated using voice controls. They can also be controlled using an app on a smartphone or a tablet.

TP-LINK Kasa

TP-LINK

★★★☆★ 327

"Alexa, turn on the coffee maker"

Smart plugs have to be installed and powered On in order for apps and Alexa to be able to communicate with them. Once they have been set up, there is a green light on the smart plug that indicates that the plug is powered On and is connected to the required wireless network.

11 Entertainment

This chapter introduces how to use the Fire TV stick.

Using the Fire TV Stick

Alexa is not just an invaluable companion on Echo devices; it can also be used to control and manage your TV. With Amazon Prime Video and the Amazon Fire TV stick, you can use voice commands to access movies and TV shows and perform a range of actions. The Amazon Fire TV stick provides access to Amazon Prime Video, and it can be controlled by a variety of devices. To use Alexa and the Fire TV stick:

Don't forget

The Fire TV stick has to be connected to your home Wi-Fi network in order to be able to access Prime Video. This is done once the Fire TV stick has been inserted into the TV's HDMI (High-Definition Multimedia Interface) slot. Follow the onscreen instructions to set up the Fire TV stick and connect it to your home Wi-Fi network.

1 The Amazon Fire TV stick can be bought from the Amazon website. Plug it into one of the HDMI slots at the back of your TV

2 The Fire TV stick comes with its own remote control, which can be used to manage the onscreen content. It can also be used with Alexa, using the button at the top of the remote control – see next page. Use these controls to manually manage content in Prime Video, via the Fire TV stick

Alexa and the Fire TV Stick

The remote control that comes with the Fire TV stick can be used with Alexa to control Prime Video content with voice commands. To do this:

1 Press and hold on this button at the top of the Fire TV stick remote control

2 While the button in Step 1 is held down, give Alexa a command, such as: "Alexa, show me all of the movies with snow in the title". From the results, an item can be played using the relevant command for Alexa, while holding down the button in Step 1 – e.g.: "Alexa, play Snow White and The Seven Dwarfs"

3 Alexa can be used to access a wide range of content using the Fire TV stick remote – e.g. say: "Alexa, show me all of the top comedy movies"

Hot tip

Alexa can also be used on the Fire TV stick to show the latest news updates, with the voice command "Alexa, play my flash briefing". This will play a video clip of the items that have been specified for your Flash Briefing update.

Linking Devices

As well as using Alexa with the Fire TV remote control, it is also possible to use Alexa on an Echo device to control Prime Video. through the Fire TV stick. To do this:

The devices to be linked have to have been set up, but they do not have to be turned on or online in order to be linked to the Fire TV stick.

1 Open the Alexa app and tap on the **Menu** button. Select **Settings** > **TV & Video**

TV & Video

2 Tap on the item you want to link so that it can be controlled by Alexa

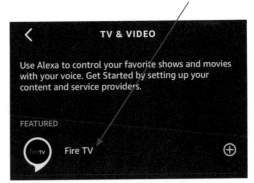

3 Tap on the **Link Your Alexa Device** button

4 Tap on the item with which you want Alexa to be linked – e.g. the Fire TV stick

5 Tap on the **Continue** button

6 Tap on the device to be linked with the Fire TV stick – i.e. the one that will be used with Alexa to send commands to the Fire TV stick

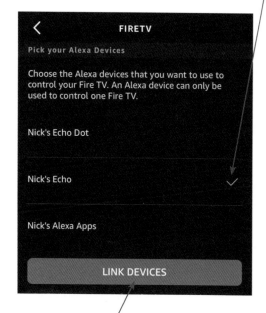

7 Tap on the **Link Devices** button

If you are going to be using Alexa on the remote control for the Fire TV stick, do not link another device in the same room, otherwise there could be some confusion between devices when you make a voice command.

...cont'd

8 The details of the linked device are displayed. Tap on the **Link Another Device** button to link another Echo device to be used with the Fire TV stick

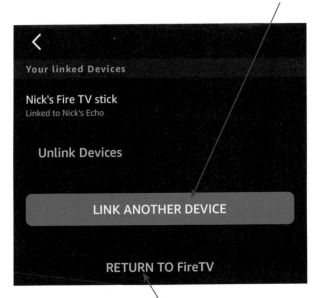

9 Tap on the **Return to FireTV** button to view suggestions for using the Echo device with the Fire TV stick

Don't forget

Tap on the **Manage devices** button in Step 9 to view details about the linked devices and add new ones, if required.

12 Help and Security

This chapter highlights some of the security issues with using Alexa.

Always Listening

Since Alexa and Echo devices are increasingly becoming integral elements in our homes, it is easy to take them for granted and forget they are there. However, even if Alexa is inactive, it does not mean nothing is going on: Alexa is there in the background, even when you are not making any voice commands.

Digital voice assistants like Alexa work by listening to your conversations and waiting for the designated "wake word". Alexa will then act on the command that comes after the wake word. Alexa will also record commands that are preceded by the wake word, and store the information that it hears on an Amazon computer (server). Since Alexa is always ready to respond to commands, it means that it is always listening, and just waiting until it hears the wake word. Therefore, in theory, it hears everything else too.

Since Alexa is always listening, it can cause some issues if it thinks it has heard a wake word when that has not been the case. There have been some instances where a digital voice assistant has misinterpreted a conversation, thinking that it contains the wake word, and actioned a request that was not actually made. Although this is a rare occurrence, it is important to remember that Alexa is always listening and to bear this in mind if you are discussing sensitive information, such as personal financial details. Some areas of conversation to consider are:

- Personal information and details relating to your family members and friends.

- Financial information, such as bank account details.

- Passwords and PIN codes for online websites, and also physical items such as bank credit and debit cards.

- Anything you would not feel comfortable with if it were distributed to a wider audience.

Beware

If you are worried about divulging sensitive information, turn off Alexa before you have a conversation about a particular subject.

It is possible to view details of everything that Alexa has recorded, and delete voice recordings as required. To do this:

1 Open the Alexa app and access **Menu** > **Settings**

2 Tap on the **Alexa Privacy** button

3 Tap on the **Review Voice History** button

Review Voice History

4 Options for controlling voice recordings are displayed

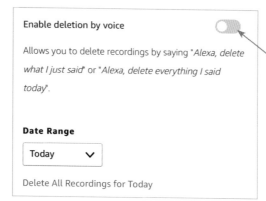

Enable deletion by voice

Allows you to delete recordings by saying *"Alexa, delete what I just said"* or *"Alexa, delete everything I said today"*.

Date Range

Today ⌄

Delete All Recordings for Today

Hot tip

Drag the **Enable deletion by voice** button **On** in Step 4 to be able to delete recordings by giving a voice command to Alexa.

181

5 Tap on a command to view its details. Tap on the **Play** button to listen to the recording

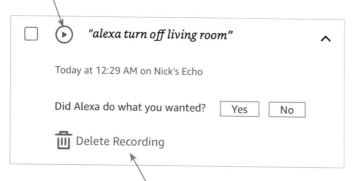

☐ ⏵ *"alexa turn off living room"* ⌃

Today at 12:29 AM on Nick's Echo

Did Alexa do what you wanted?   Yes   No

🗑 Delete Recording

6 Tap on the **Delete Recording** button to remove the recorded data from the Amazon server

Looking for Help

The Alexa app is an invaluable source of helpful information in relation to both Alexa and Echo devices. To access some of the help functions:

Hot tip

Alexa can also be a good source of help if you want to ask a question directly. To do this, ask Alexa a question such as: "Alexa, how do I change the wake word?". Alexa will provide the answer, if possible. The answer will also be shown on the **Menu > Activity** page in the Alexa app.

1 Open the Alexa app, tap on the **Menu** button, and tap on the **Help & Feedback** button

2 In the **Help & Feedback** section, tap on one of the main categories to view the sub-categories within it. There are also options to send an email and send feedback

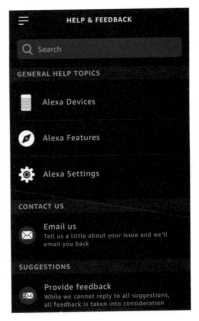

3 Navigate through the sub-categories until you find the required topic. Tap on the topic to view the full details

More Help Options

The Things to Try section of the Alexa app not only has suggestions about how to use Alexa on an Echo device, but also help information about each topic. To use this:

1 Open the Alexa app, tap on the **Menu** button, and tap on the **Things to Try** button

2 Tap on one of the main **Things to Try** categories to view the sub-categories within it

The Things to Try section is a great way to see the wide range of options that are available with Alexa.

3 Tap on the topic to view the full details

...cont'd

4 Each category or sub-category has relevant suggestions for voice commands to give Alexa

Only some of the Things to Try categories have a **Learn more** option.

5 Swipe down to the bottom of the screen and tap on the **Learn more** button, if there is one, to find out more information about the selected topic

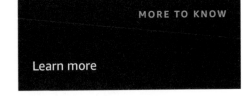

6 Tap on one of the links for one of the help topics for the selected category to view more details about it

Troubleshooting

Connection problems

Some of the issues that may occur are:

- The Echo does not connect to your home Wi-Fi network. Check on another device to see if it can connect to the Wi-Fi router in the usual way. If it is an issue just with the Echo, there are a number of troubleshooting options to try: move the Echo nearer to the router to see if the issue is being too far away to pick up a strong signal; reset the router and try connecting the Echo again; or check in the Wi-Fi settings of the Alexa app: **Menu** > **Settings** > **Device Settings** > **[Echo name]** > **Wi-Fi Network** and tap on the **Change** button to set up Wi-Fi on the Echo device again.

Beware

Wi-Fi Network
PLUSNET-TXJ5-5g   Change

- The Echo does not connect to an external Bluetooth device. Make sure the device itself is in pairing mode so that the Echo can find it. In the Alexa app, go to **Menu** > **Settings** > **Device Settings** > **[Echo name]** > **Bluetooth Devices** and tap on the **Pair a New Device** button. If the device is still not recognized, move it closer to the Echo and retry.

If Alexa does not respond when you issue an instruction, this could be due to a faulty power connection. Check the Echo plug at the wall socket and ensure it is turned On. Also, check the cable to ensure it is not damaged, or has been pulled loose from the Echo at any time – e.g. when furniture is being moved around.

Bluetooth Settings

Select a previously paired device.

Paired Devices

Bluetooth SoundCore mini   ⌄

PAIR A NEW DEVICE

...cont'd

Beware

If Alexa has problems recognizing your voice commands, make sure that the Echo is in a good location: away from walls, not on the floor, and clear of any devices that could cause interference, such as microwave ovens. After giving a command, check what Alexa heard by tapping on **Menu > Activity** in the Alexa app. Tap on the **More** button to see exactly what Alexa heard. Tap on the **Learn more** button to view additional options.

Hot tip

To use another speaker with Alexa, such as a Bluetooth one, tap on the **Change** button next to the **Speaker** option in the **Device Settings** window. Tap on the required speaker and tap on the **Save** button.

Sound problems

Generally, if you treat your Echo well, there will not be too many problems with the sound. However, there are some issues that could arise, and they include:

- **There is no sound from the Echo**. Check that the volume has not been turned down with the decrease volume button on the top of the Echo.

- **Sounds for alarms, timers or notifications cannot be heard**. In the Alexa app, go to **Menu > Settings > Device Settings > [Echo name]**. The sound settings for the device are displayed. Tap on the **Audio Settings** option to check the bass, midrange and treble for the speakers.

- **Alexa cannot hear you at all**. Check that the microphone on the Echo has not been turned off. This is done by pressing the microphone button on the top of the Echo. If the microphone is off, the button and the light ring at the top of the Echo turn red. Press the microphone button to turn it back on.

Index